CHASING VINES

GROUP EXPERIENCE

BETH MOORE

WITH KARIN STOCK BUURSMA

chasing vines

Finding your way to
an immensely fruitful life

TYNDALE
MOMENTUM®

The Tyndale nonfiction imprint

Visit Tyndale online at tyndale.com.

Visit Tyndale Momentum online at tyndalemomentum.com.

Visit Beth Moore online at lproof.org.

TYNDALE, Tyndale's quill logo, *Tyndale Momentum*, and the Tyndale Momentum logo are registered trademarks of Tyndale House Ministries. Tyndale Momentum is the nonfiction imprint of Tyndale House Publishers, Carol Stream, Illinois.

Designed by Dean H. Renninger

Edited by Stephanie Rische

Published in association with Yates & Yates, LLP (yates2.com).

For information about special discounts for bulk purchases, please contact Tyndale House Publishers at csresponse@tyndale.com, or call 1-800-323-9400.

ISBN 978-1-4964-4088-4

Printed in the United States of America

26 25 24 23 22 21
10   9   8   7   6   5

CONTENTS

To Cindy:

I can give no higher compliment to anyone than to say
you increased our love for the true Vine. We will be forever
grateful for your hospitality and, even more so, for your faith.
We will love you, your family, and your vineyards all our lives.

For the love of the Vine,

Beth

A NOTE TO LEADERS

Thank you for investing your time into leading a group through the *Chasing Vines Group Experience*. I pray that it will be a meaningful time for all of you as you meet together to read, discuss, and pray about what it means to abide in Christ and live fruitful lives. You are my partner in this journey, and I am deeply grateful for you. I am praying for you and those you lead!

Here are a few suggestions to help your group run smoothly:

- The study is designed to be done over six sessions. We recommend that groups meet for an hour minimum per gathering to get the most out of the experience. Here is your weekly rhythm:

    Group Gathering:
    Discuss the questions from the previous week.
    Watch the DVD message for that session.
    As time permits, discuss anything notable in the message. (optional)
    Close in prayer.

    On Your Own:
    Read the assigned part of *Chasing Vines*.
    Complete homework (or as much as possible) before the next gathering.

    Repeat until your final gathering for session 6!

- Before your group meets each session, ask God to direct your discussion in a way that honors Him and benefits all the participants.
- Encourage those in your group to read the designated chapters in *Chasing Vines* and work through the study on their own before you meet. The discussion will be deeper and more meaningful if everyone is prepared.
- If you find you don't have time to get through all the material in one meeting, choose a few specific areas to focus on. You could pick one of the two "Planting the Seed" sections to work through first, adding the second if you have time.
- Include a time of prayer at the end of the meeting. Encourage your group members to pray for one another throughout the week.
- Encourage your group members to choose one or two of the application suggestions at the end of each session's study. You might follow up the next week and ask participants to share their experiences.

The Vineyard

The Lord God planted a garden.

GENESIS 2:8

Meet with your group and watch session 1 of the DVD before you begin reading *Chasing Vines*. This is your introduction to the entire experience you have ahead. I want to officially welcome you!

GROUP GATHERING

Discussion: Leader, invite participants to share what has drawn them to *Chasing Vines* and the group experience.

Watch session 1 of the DVD. Use the Listening Guide as you view the message.

— Listening Guide —

1. What is the goal for this book and the coinciding journey? (Fill in the blanks.)

For every reader, without exception, to _____ with Jesus and grow in _____ in a way that results in _____ fruit bearing.

2. *Why is living a fruitful life in Christ a priority? (Fill in the blanks.)*

- Your fruitfulness brings direct _____.
- Your fruitfulness brings direct _____.
- Your fruitfulness brings both direct and indirect _____.
- Your fruitfulness brings _____.
- Your fruitfulness brings _____, who hoped to

  _____.

3. *What is your hope and desire for fruitfulness? What do you want to get out of this* Chasing Vines *experience?*

_____

_____

_____

_____

Read Colossians 1:1-12. Personalize it into the following petition, to be prayed often in the pursuit of an immensely fruitful life.

_____, that I may be filled with the knowledge of Your will in all wisdom and spiritual understanding, so that I may walk worthy of You, Lord, fully pleasing to You: _____ and growing in the knowledge of God, being strengthened with all power, according to Your glorious might, so that I may have great _____ and patience, _____ to You, my Father, who have enabled me to share in the saints of inheritance in the light. _____ from the domain of darkness and transferred me into the Kingdom of Your Son whom You love. (Taken from Colossians 1:9-13, CSB)

— *Prayer* —

Take some time to share concerns with your group and pray together. Thank God for His tender care and for the process of growing in faith. Ask Him to help you see beauty in the slow and sometimes difficult growing process, and to trust that He is at work in your life. Ask Him for grace to be fruitful wherever you are planted and for faith to find your truest place in Him.

✦ ✦ ✦

ON YOUR OWN

During the week, read the introduction and part 1 ("The Vineyard") of *Chasing Vines*. Then proceed with "A Word from Beth" and this week's homework. Resist thinking of the homework as drudgery! This isn't high school. This is the high calling! Pray that God will help you love every minute of it, because none of it will be wasted. God will use it to increase both His glory and your fruitfulness.

— A Word from Beth —

If there's one thing I want to say to you as you get started on this study, it's this: God made you to contribute to His Kingdom in a way only you can. This is true whether you're a superachiever who seems to have it all together or someone who feels like you are one mishap away from losing your grip on life. You are a child of God, loved by Him and created by Him for a purpose.

That's the foundational truth we're going to build on in this study. And yet, as much as we may know it, we don't always feel it. As I write in the introduction to *Chasing Vines*, "I know what it's like to fear not being seen. I know what it's like to worry that I'm not of use. I know how easy it is to feel gift-less in a gift-driven society." I'm pretty sure I'm not alone in this. We long for our lives to make an impact, even if we're not sure how.

The focus of this book—and of our lives—is being fruitful. But the fruit itself is not always the point. God Himself seems to consider the process of growing to be almost as important as the fruit.

If you're a gardener, you understand this. You may have tended your own tomato plants, like I did with Keith and his parents, and watched with excitement as the fruit first appeared and then grew bit by bit. You might know the joy of seeing green begin to turn orange and the sheer delight of feasting on the first ripe tomato with dirt still on it. The fruit is all the more delicious when we've seen it grow. When we've tended something with our own hands. When we know the obstacles that have been overcome. When we see the beautiful end that we could hardly imagine at the beginning.

Our growth is important to God—and He plants us in just the right spot.

Planting the Seed

Note to leaders: You'll see that I have selected several questions that might be especially good for discussion in your next group gathering, but feel free to select ones you prefer!

GROWTH

In a book about fruitfulness, it makes sense that everything begins with dirt, because that's where all fruit begins. In chapter 1, I write, "It is a poor soul who confuses dirt with filth or soil with soiled. . . . The fact is, in the hands of the consummate Potter, dirt is fodder for His wheel."

1. How does a gardener look at dirt differently from someone who isn't a gardener? How might we look at our lives differently if we saw the less savory parts from the Gardener's perspective?

_____

_____

_____

_____

2. The word human *means "a creature of earth," so perhaps it's not surprising that Genesis recounts that the first human was made from dirt. In chapter 1, I write,*

> We could imagine the Creator with arms long enough to keep
> His face from getting dusty through the whole creative ordeal, but
> blowing breath into the human's nostrils sketches a different posture.

Here we have a Maker leaning low, near to the ground. Here we have God who is high and lifted up but is now bending over, animating dust. God, mouth-to-nose with man.

3. *Consider this image of God bending low, getting close enough to breathe life into Adam. What does this description show us about God and about the relationship He wants to have with us?*

The creation account in Genesis 2, which fills in some details that are missing in Genesis 1, says, "The LORD God planted a garden in Eden." In John 15:1, we see Jesus telling the disciples, "My Father is the gardener" (CSB). That's a surprising image to some of us. We're more likely to think of God as Creator or King—as One who used His power to set the stars in place, create the roaring oceans, and order the universe. But a gardener is someone who tends. One who sees. One who plans—and plants.

In chapter 1, I write,

> The reason planting is so crucial to appreciating the process is because it is spectacularly deliberate. In life, so many unexplainable things happen that can make a person feel like everything is one enormous accident. . . .
>
> We long for continuity, for some semblance of purpose—anything that might suggest we're on the right track. Instead, we feel like ashes, leftovers from a bygone fire, blown aimlessly by the wind. . . .
>
> Our perceptions can be very convincing, but God tells us the truth. Nothing about our existence is accidental. We were known before we knew we were alive. We were planned and, as a matter of fact, *planted* on this earth for this moment in time.

4. *What kinds of deliberate steps are involved in planting? Have there been times in your life when you felt like an accident? How might this idea of God deliberately planting you inform your view of who you are and why you're here?*

_____

_____

_____

_____

Read Psalm 92:12-15, which gives us a glimpse of what it's like to be planted by God.

> The righteous flourish like the palm tree
>   and grow like a cedar in Lebanon.
> They are planted in the house of the LORD;
>   they flourish in the courts of our God.
> They still bear fruit in old age;
>   they are ever full of sap and green,
> to declare that the LORD is upright;
>   he is my rock, and there is no unrighteousness in him.

5. *Where are the righteous planted? What does this passage say is true about them? What is their ultimate goal?*

_____

_____

_____

_____

Here's a fact you can rely on: If God plants you, He will tend you. He is not the kind of gardener who gets bored and forgets to water His plants. He is not the kind of gardener who will walk away and let His plants die. He knows exactly how much sun, water, and fertilizer each plant needs. And He knows how to make the plants in His garden thrive.

Gardening takes time. Flowers don't bloom immediately, fruit takes a while to form, trees take years to mature and deepen their roots, and the gardener must put forth patient effort to help His plants to thrive.

So when we think of ourselves as plants, it raises some questions. Why does the omnipotent God choose to use this slow and sometimes painful process to bring us to full maturity and fruitfulness?

In chapter 1, I write,

> It's a wonder that God would choose to slowly grow what He could have simply created grown. Why on earth would He go to the trouble to plant a garden forced to sprout rather than commanding it into existence, full bloom? Why leave His desk and get His pant legs soiled?
> Because God likes watching things grow.

6. *Why do you think God uses this slow process to shape us? What slow-growing fruit have you seen in your life? How do you think the results would have been different if they had come quickly, without struggle?*

_____

_____

_____

_____

7. *What qualities, characteristics, or service do you think might be sprouting in your life now? What kind of cultivation might they need?*

_____

_____

_____

_____

It's reassuring to me that we are not wildflowers (or weeds!) that have sprung up in a field or forest. We are plants in a garden—put there deliberately and cultivated by a gardener who knows what He is doing. And He is working on us—preparing the soil, removing weeds and other obstacles, giving us the sun and water and air we need to thrive. He knows the conditions we need so we can bear the biggest, tastiest, most beautiful fruit.

God, the master Gardener, is working even when we can't see Him.

8. *What helps you to trust that God is cultivating fruit in your life even when you're not sure you see it?*

_____

_____

_____

_____

Read Psalm 77:11-19, where the psalmist is reminding himself of all God did for his ancestors when they escaped from slavery in Egypt and passed through the Red Sea.

I will remember the deeds of the LORD;
　　yes, I will remember your wonders of old.
I will ponder all your work,
　　and meditate on your mighty deeds.
Your way, O God, is holy.
　　What god is great like our God?
You are the God who works wonders;
　　you have made known your might among the peoples.
You with your arm redeemed your people,
　　the children of Jacob and Joseph.

When the waters saw you, O God,
　　when the waters saw you, they were afraid;
　　indeed, the deep trembled.
The clouds poured out water;
　　the skies gave forth thunder;
　　your arrows flashed on every side.
The crash of your thunder was in the whirlwind;

your lightnings lighted up the world;
   the earth trembled and shook.

Your way was through the sea,
   your path through the great waters;
      yet your footprints were unseen.

List some of the things the Lord did for the Israelites. How does remembering God's faithfulness in the past help us trust Him for the future? What are some tangible ways we could remember God's faithfulness—to us personally, to figures in the Bible, and to those in our church family and others we know?

The psalmist talks about God guiding the people through the Red Sea, yet His "footprints were unseen." I love this image of invisible footprints leading the way. The Israelites could see the water parting, but they couldn't see God Himself. Even the pillar of cloud, which had been leading them through the desert, moved behind them to shield them from the Egyptians. One of the Israelites had to take the first step into the parted waters.

9. *Imagine being one of the Israelites by the Red Sea, seemingly trapped between the Egyptian army and the water. How might you have reacted when the water parted? Would you have had the faith to move forward?*

_____

_____

_____

10. *Where might God be working in your life even though His footprints are unseen to you right now?*

_____

_____

_____

God's work in us is sometimes invisible—and always takes time.

Have you ever wondered why God goes to the trouble of sanctifying us? He could instantly zap us into His image the moment we decide to follow Jesus, or He could transport us into heaven the moment of our conversion. Why would He opt for taking us through the long, drawn-out process of planting, watering, pruning, and harvesting? But sure enough, He rolls up His sleeves, puts palms to the dirt, and begins putting the pieces of our lives together in a way that matters.

I think it's because He's not looking for a store-bought tomato. He wants the real thing, raised by His own hands, hard won as it is.

To a gardener, grown is overrated. It's growing it that makes the fruit sweet.

11. Have you ever experienced this kind of joy over a project you have seen through from start to finish? What is satisfying about seeing the fruit of your labors? How does your reaction change when the growth process was especially difficult?

There are two parts to our salvation. Scripture is clear that justification—becoming right in God's sight—comes right away when we trust in Jesus' sacrifice to save us. Read Romans 10:9 and 2 Corinthians 5:17.

If you confess with your mouth that Jesus is Lord and believe in your heart that God raised him from the dead, you will be saved.

Therefore, if anyone is in Christ, he is a new creation. The old has passed away; behold, the new has come.

12. What transformation occurs when we trust in Christ and confess Him as Lord?

_____

_____

_____

_____

Sanctification—the process of becoming more like Jesus—takes time. In fact, it won't be complete until we are with God and we fully become the people He created us to be.

Read 1 John 3:2.

Dear friends, we are already God's children, but he has not yet shown us what we will be like when Christ appears. But we do know that we will be like him, for we will see him as he really is. (NLT)

13. *How does this verse highlight the tension between the "already and not yet"—what we are now and what we will eventually become?*

_____

_____

_____

_____

Read Ephesians 4:13-15.

This [teaching] will continue until we all come to such unity in our faith and knowledge of God's Son that we will be mature in the Lord, measuring up to the full and complete standard of Christ. Then we will no longer be immature like children. We won't be tossed and blown about by every wind of new teaching. We will not be influenced when people try to trick us with lies so clever they sound like the truth. Instead, we will speak the truth in love, growing in every way more and more like Christ, who is the head of his body, the church. (NLT)

14. *Based on this passage, how would you describe the process of sanctification? What is its ultimate goal?*

_____

_____

_____

_____

15. Why do you think God makes sanctification a process rather than a single moment? What are the benefits of this process?

_____

_____

_____

_____

Read Philippians 1:6.

I am sure of this, that he who began a good work in you will bring it to completion at the day of Jesus Christ.

16. What work are you grateful that God will be faithful to complete in you?

_____

_____

_____

_____

PLACE

If we're thinking of ourselves as plants in this gardening metaphor, one of the most basic questions we face is, Where are we planted? What's our *terroir*, our sense of place? In chapter 2, I write about trying to find a place where I belong but never quite being able to do it.

> After countless conversations, I've come to the conclusion that what most of us have in common is the feeling that we're misfits.
>
> I've also been told a few times to stay in my place. I wanted to respond, "I'd be more than happy to, if I could just figure out where on earth my place is."
>
> Maybe nothing is more normal than feeling a bit abnormal. Maybe feeling comfortable in our own skin means coming to the realization that we weren't created to feel particularly comfortable in this skin.

1. *Most of us can relate to this feeling that we don't quite fit in. Why do you think that is? When in your life have you been most bothered by this feeling?*

_____

_____

_____

In chapter 2, we look in depth at Psalm 80, which presents the image of the people of Israel as a vine God brought out of Egypt and transplanted to the Promised Land. At first it thrived. Then things began to change.

Read Psalm 80:7-13.

Restore us, O God of hosts;
    let your face shine, that we may be saved!

You brought a vine out of Egypt;
    you drove out the nations and planted it.
You cleared the ground for it;
    it took deep root and filled the land.
The mountains were covered with its shade,
    the mighty cedars with its branches.
It sent out its branches to the sea
    and its shoots to the River.
Why then have you broken down its walls,
    so that all who pass along the way
        pluck its fruit?
The boar from the forest ravages it,
    and all that move in the field feed on it.

2. *How did the vine grow at first? What do these lavish descriptions suggest? Now what has happened to the vine? Why?*

_____

_____

_____

While we don't know the precise historical context for what was going on in this psalm, there are enough descriptions throughout Scripture of Israel's unfaithfulness to God to give us an idea. The people thrived when they followed the Lord, but all too often they turned to idols, following the pagan practices of the nations around them. They did what seemed right to them, forgetting that God had planted them in a specific place for a specific purpose. They were not there by accident—and neither are we. We, too, are chosen to be His children.

In chapter 2, I write,

> He didn't choose you because you happened to be in the right place at the right time or because nobody better was in arm's reach. God's arm is neither short nor weak (Isaiah 59:1). No one is out of His reach. If He chose you, He did so on purpose.

Read Ephesians 1:3-4.

> Blessed be the God and Father of our Lord Jesus Christ, who has blessed us in Christ with every spiritual blessing in the heavenly places, even as he chose us in him before the foundation of the world, that we should be holy and blameless before him.

3. *When did God choose us? Why is this significant? What did He choose us for?*

_____

_____

_____

_____

Read 1 Peter 2:9.

> You are a chosen race, a royal priesthood, a holy nation, a people for his own possession, that you may proclaim the excellencies of him who called you out of darkness into his marvelous light.

4. *How does this verse describe believers? For what purpose have we been chosen?*

_____

_____

_____

_____

5. *Where has God chosen to plant you right now?*

_____

_____

_____

_____

Years before Psalm 80 was written, the vine of Israel had been struggling in Egypt. From there, the people cried out to God for deliverance. Scripture says that He heard them: "And God knew" (Exodus 2:25).

But the phrase "And God knew" is not a simple statement of fact. Of course God knew about their plight. He knows everything; nothing is hidden from His notice. "And God knew" means that He knew what would happen. He knew how He would act on the Israelites' behalf. He knew the joyful future they could not see.

God knew that slavery wasn't the end of His people's story. He knew the enemy wouldn't get the final victory. He knew He would keep His promises in dramatic fashion. He had delivered them before, and He would deliver them again. . . .

God transplanted the vine—He snatched it right out of the ground and carried it out of Egypt, with four centuries of roots dangling, so He could plant it back in the soil of its belonging. Its home. Its true terroir.

6. *What might God "know" about you in this sense? What are you struggling with that will not be the end of your story?*

_____

_____

God's action in this case was to transplant His people. He had sustained them in their oppression for many years, but now He took them out of their suffering and moved them to a place where they could flourish.

It wasn't easy being transplanted after four hundred years. The Israelites had to form new roots that would grow down deep into new soil. At times it was painful. They worried that God had brought them into the desert to die. (He hadn't.) They complained that they were going to die of thirst. (They didn't.) They complained that they had no food to eat. (They did—food straight from God's hand.) They didn't trust God, so they turned to idols. And as we talked about last week, when they reached the Promised Land that God had prepared for them, most of them didn't believe they could defeat the Canaanites who lived there.

But a few generations later, one transplanted Israelite family produced a young boy named Samuel, who would become a great prophet of God. Later, another family produced a boy named David, who became king, wrote beautiful psalms, and became known as a man after God's own heart.

Transplanting, like growing, takes time. Time for new roots to form and function. Time to get used to new soil, new rain patterns, new climate. And yet, when we're transplanted, we know that the master Gardener has put us in our new place for a purpose. He understands the conditions we experienced before and the new ones we're facing now. We can trust that His goal is always our flourishing and our fruitfulness.

7. *Do you feel like you've been transplanted? What might be a reason for the change?*

_____

_____

_____

_____

Sometimes transplanting involves taking us out of something that was harmful for us. Sometimes it has to do with planting us somewhere that will be beneficial for us. Sometimes it's both. Other times transplanting us might help someone else—a new neighbor, a new friend or acquaintance, someone who sees our faith as we try to put down roots in a new situation.

8. *What are some of the challenges that come with being transplanted? What can be the benefits? How can we exhibit faith during a time of transition?*

_____

_____

_____

_____

It's interesting to note that although God transplanted the Israelites so they could be more fruitful, that doesn't mean their vines were bare in Egypt. Even in tough growing conditions, they produced fruit.

Read Genesis 41:51-52.

Joseph called the name of the firstborn Manasseh. "For," he said, "God has made me forget all my hardship and all my father's house." The name of the second he called Ephraim, "For God has made me fruitful in the land of my affliction."

9. *What does the name Ephraim mean?*

_____

_____

_____

_____

Maybe you wish God would transplant you, but for now He's keeping you right where you are. Maybe you would like a fresh start, better soil, more sunlight, but for the time being you are dealing with rocky ground and too much rain. Don't give up! God can produce fruit in you even in these conditions. Even in the land of your affliction.

Never confuse fruitfulness with felicity. That's not to say that fruit bearing can't be fun. But equate the two—fruitfulness and fun—and you'll miss some of your most fertile opportunities to bear inexplicable fruit.

10. When have times of affliction brought fruitfulness in your life?

_____

_____

_____

_____

We read story after story in the Bible of people who felt out of place. They may have wished that God would transplant them somewhere else where they would finally fit in and feel at home. And yet God uses their stories to speak to us in our own sense of isolation or discomfort.

11. Choose one or two people from the list below and discuss how they were able to be fruitful even when they felt out of place. What kind of fruit did they bear?
- *Abraham:* He moved away from his family and his culture to follow a God he didn't even know. (See Genesis 12:1-8.)
- *Esther:* She found herself queen of a pagan empire and separated from anyone else who shared her faith. In fact, she was instructed to tell no one about her Jewish heritage. (See Esther 2:1-10; 15-20.)
- *David:* When Saul was trying to kill him, David had to run away and live in the wilderness to escape. (See 1 Samuel 19:1-17; Psalm 57.)
- *The woman who anointed Jesus with oil:* She found herself the object of scorn in a room full of men. (See Matthew 26:6-13.)

_____

_____

_____

_____

All of these people—and many more—struggled, but their stories still speak to us. Abraham's faith became the prime example of what it means to trust God and step out in faith. Esther's lonely position in the palace allowed her to save her people. David's need to run from Saul bolstered his dependence on God and led him to write psalms that still encourage us today. And the woman who anointed

Jesus became an example of what it looks like when we love Him more than our own reputations. They were fruitful where they were, even while they longed for their true place.

It's not a coincidence that so many of us feel like misfits in this world. That's because this world is not our home, and our true place is not here.

Nothing haunts us more than our search for, finally, a sense of place. As it turns out, true belonging is found only in the sovereign palm of God. There alone we find our place, even amid the seasons of moving, planting, uprooting, and replanting.

It's only when we find our place in Him that we find rest.

Read Psalm 91:1-2, which points us to our true home.

Those who live in the shelter of the Most High
    will find rest in the shadow of the Almighty.
This I declare about the LORD:
He alone is my refuge, my place of safety;
    he is my God, and I trust him. (NLT)

12. What words does the psalmist use to describe God?

_____

_____

_____

13. Resting involves stopping whatever else we're doing—worrying, striving, strategizing. How do we exhibit trust when we find rest in God?

_____

_____

_____

_____

Several New Testament passages talk about the true home we will have in heaven. Read Ephesians 2:19-20.

> You are no longer foreigners and strangers, but fellow citizens with God's people and also members of his household, built on the foundation of the apostles and prophets, with Christ Jesus himself as the chief cornerstone. (NIV)

14. *What was our old identity? How does Paul describe our new identity?*

_____

_____

_____

_____

15. *What are the implications of our true citizenship being in heaven, with God?*
   What might become more or less important to us if we remembered this truth?

_____

_____

_____

_____

Hebrews 11, the great "hall of faith" chapter, talks about myriad Old Testament figures who lived by faith. Read Hebrews 11:13-16.

> All these people died still believing what God had promised them. They did not receive what was promised, but they saw it all from a distance and welcomed it. They agreed that they were foreigners and nomads here on earth. Obviously people who say such things are looking forward to a country they can call their own. If they had longed for the country they came from, they could have gone back. But they were looking for a better place, a heavenly homeland. That is why God is not ashamed to be called their God, for he has prepared a city for them. (NLT)

16. The writer of Hebrews calls these people "foreigners and nomads here on earth." What are some characteristics of foreigners and nomads? How do these descriptions apply to us as believers?

_____

_____

_____

_____

_____

When you find yourself feeling out of place and like you don't belong, let it be a moment of encouragement. This doesn't mean there's something wrong with you. Instead, it means you were created for someplace else. When we feel that sense of longing, we can embrace it—because it's pointing us to our true terroir, our ultimate place, our home.

— Wrapping Up —

Let's close our time together with these words from 1 Corinthians 13:12:

Now we see in a mirror dimly, but then face to face. Now I know in part;
then I shall know fully, even as I have been fully known.

This verse is the key to our truest sense of place, isn't it? A place where we understand fully—and where we ourselves will be fully known and understood by God. A place where we don't have to hide any part of ourselves, where we don't have to worry about whether we're like those around us but can be truly ourselves.

This is a promise for the future, but parts of it are realized right now. God knows us fully; we don't have to hide any aspect of ourselves from Him. And through His planting, His cultivating, His transplanting, His intimate knowledge of us, He is making us more fruitful. As we become more like Him, we become more the people we were created to be—and we become more and more at home in our true place.

— *Deepening Our Roots* —

On your own this week, try one or two of these activities:

- Take a few minutes to think about the person you were a year or two ago. How have you changed? What growth have you seen? What have you learned in the process?
- This week, identify a person or two in your group whom you have seen be fruitful in the midst of affliction. Write them a note to tell them what you've observed and encourage them to persevere.
- In a journal, write about your own sense of place. Where do you feel you belong? When do you struggle to feel rooted and secure? How might you lean in to the idea that God is your true place?
- Write Psalm 92:12-15 on an index card and place it where you will see it every day. (You can also text it to yourself or put it in your digital calendar so it will pop up on your phone periodically.) Meditate on what it means to be planted in the house of God.

The Vinedresser

Let me sing for my beloved my love song concerning his vineyard:
My beloved had a vineyard on a very fertile hill.

ISAIAH 5:1

GROUP GATHERING

Discussion: As a group, discuss your answers to the selected questions in the previous "On Your Own" section based on part 1, "The Vineyard."

Watch session 2 of the DVD.

— *Listening Guide* —

1. Our Vinedresser's entire approach to gardening is _____ and _____.

2. How easy or hard is it for you to believe that, like Lalou Bize-Leroy's vines, you are well loved—that God really understands and cares when you're not doing well?

_____

_____

_____

— *Prayer* —

Take some time to share concerns with your group and pray together. Ask God for the courage to inspect your fruit and the discernment to see what is good and what needs to change. Thank God that He is using the rocks in our lives to produce good fruit. Ask Him to help you trust Him more deeply in the midst of your struggles.

+   +   +

ON YOUR OWN

During the week, read part 2 ("The Vinedresser") of *Chasing Vines.* Then proceed with "A Word from Beth" and this week's homework.

— *A Word from Beth* —

In the second part of *Chasing Vines*, "The Vinedresser," we look at who God is and the ways He prepares us for lives of fruitfulness. He chooses the field, digs it up, clears it, removes some of the stones, and plants the vines. The master Gardener does nothing by accident, so we can be sure that any obstacles that remain are there to help us bear more and better fruit.

If our lives are about bearing fruit—if that's one of the things that gives our lives meaning and purpose—then we want to bear *good* fruit.

Sometimes the difference between good fruit and bad fruit is glaringly obvious—maybe especially when that fruit belongs to someone else. Other people's failures are often easy to see, and the sad fact is that we sometimes find a little too much pleasure in pointing them out. But evaluating our own fruit? That can be another story.

Inspecting our own fruit is critical if we want to become more fruitful. And the thing is, we don't have to cringe when we do this. Inspection shows us what is wrong in our lives, but it also shows us what is good. There is a kind of beauty in honest evaluation.

In my conversation with Cindy, the vineyard owner, she talks about the dangers of bleeding inward and how we need to open our hearts and lives to the work of the

Vinedresser. Of course, by no means is all woundedness related to a spiritual deficit or a lack of faith. But in order to be healthy—spiritually and otherwise—we need to be rooted in Christ, the source of true life.

— Planting the Seed —

INSPECTION

At the beginning of chapter 5, I tell about all the years I fasted during my weekend Living Proof events. God wasn't calling me to do this, but I thought a big gesture like going without food might tip the scales of God's favor in my direction. Eventually—when I almost blacked out while speaking—I figured out that even though this seemed like a good and even godly idea, it wasn't bearing good fruit in my life.

1. *When have you spent time or energy on something that God wasn't asking you to do and wasn't bearing good fruit? How did you figure out that you needed to change what you were doing?*

_____

_____

_____

_____

2. *Do you relate to the false assumption that we can earn God's favor by doing great things for Him? How does this affect your choices?*

_____

_____

_____

_____

Let's be clear that our goal in producing more and better fruit is not to move up on God's approval list or gain more of His love. As believers in Christ, we already have His love and approval. Rather, our goal is to honor God and fulfill His purposes for us.

In chapter 5, I write,

Since the Father calls Jesus-followers to live immensely fruitful lives, it stands to reason that no question is more relevant than this: What kind of fruit are we producing? We can't see fruit the way God can, but with His help, we are fully capable of distinguishing between good fruit and bad fruit. . . .

Ever since I began chasing vines in Tuscany, I've been increasingly analyzing the quality of some of the fruit coming from my own life and leadership. Would you be willing to risk making this question part of your frequent vocabulary too?

Is what I'm doing (this action, approach, example, or instruction) bearing good fruit?

3. *Is this a question you regularly consider? How might you make this a habit in your life?*

_____

_____

_____

_____

_____

It's important to reiterate the point that inspection is not just looking for what's wrong, like a demanding teacher who scrawls all over your essay with a red pen or a critical boss who reprimands you in front of your coworkers. Yes, we want to identify what needs to be changed, but we also want to identify what is already working.

In chapter 5, I write,

If we think we have a God who only convicts and never encourages, who only tells us what's wrong with us and never what's right, we've probably created a god made in the image of a human authority who scarred us. We're safe and loved by God, no matter what kind of fruit we're currently producing.

4. *Have you ever received constructive feedback—from a supervisor, a teacher, a mentor, or someone else in your life—that helped you make a course correction or change for the better?*

_____

_____

_____

5. *Why do we often assume evaluation only means pointing out what is bad?*

_____

_____

_____

Read Lamentations 3:22-23.

The steadfast love of the LORD never ceases;
    his mercies never come to an end;
they are new every morning;
    great is your faithfulness.

6. *What does this passage reveal about God? How can we remind ourselves that God is on our side and that His love and faithfulness are not dependent on our performance?*

_____

_____

_____

_____

7. *How can we tell if we're bearing good fruit?*

_____

_____

_____

Read Galatians 5:16-24.

Walk by the Spirit, and you will not gratify the desires of the flesh. For the desires of the flesh are against the Spirit, and the desires of the Spirit are against the flesh, for these are opposed to each other, to keep you from doing the things you want to do. But if you are led by the Spirit, you are not under the law. Now the works of the flesh are evident: sexual immorality, impurity, sensuality, idolatry, sorcery, enmity, strife, jealousy, fits of anger, rivalries, dissensions, divisions, envy, drunkenness, orgies, and things like these. I warn you, as I warned you before, that those who do such things will not inherit the kingdom of God. But the fruit of the Spirit is love, joy, peace, patience, kindness, goodness, faithfulness, gentleness, self-control; against such things there is no law. And those who belong to Christ Jesus have crucified the flesh with its passions and desires.

8. *Contrast the works of the flesh with the works of the Spirit. What are the goals of each? The results?*

_____

_____

_____

_____

We can often evaluate our fruit based on what it leads to. We can look at what we're leaving in our wake, whether in our own thoughts and attitudes or in our relationships. Is it dissension, selfishness, and division, or is it kindness, self-control, and patience?

9. *Which of the fruits of the Spirit have you seen grow in your life in the past few years? Which would you like to see more of?*

_____

_____

_____

_____

Read Romans 8:29.

Those whom he foreknew he also predestined to be conformed to the image of his Son, in order that he might be the firstborn among many brothers.

10. *What do you think it means to be "conformed to the image of" Jesus? How can we evaluate our fruit in this light?*

_____

_____

_____

11. *What positions of leadership or influence do you hold? What kind of fruit do you most hope to see from those positions?*

_____

_____

_____

Review this list of questions, which also appears in chapter 5 of *Chasing Vines*.

- Is my heart growing warmer or colder toward people?
- Am I constantly in a bad mood?
- Am I increasingly exhausted?
- Do I get fixated on offenses, or am I willing to overlook most of them?
- Have I become harsher or gentler over the last year?
- Do I lose control easily?

12. *Which of these questions do you find most helpful as you seek to evaluate the fruit in your own life?*

_____

_____

_____

Thinking through these questions carefully will take time and should be done independently. (We'll come back to this list at the end of the chapter as one of the activities you can do on your own.) Such reflection requires us to be honest with ourselves about our motives, our thoughts, and our attitudes. We must look not only at what happened but at how it happened; not only at what showed on the outside but also at what was going on inside. That's because our fruit isn't just about how we affect other people. It's also about whether we are holding more tightly to Jesus and looking more like Him.

In chapter 5, I talk about asking myself if I've served others straw or wheat. The apostle Paul looks at this concept in 1 Corinthians.

Read 1 Corinthians 3:10-15.

According to the grace of God given to me, like a skilled master builder I laid a foundation, and someone else is building upon it. Let each one take care how he builds upon it. For no one can lay a foundation other than that which is laid, which is Jesus Christ. Now if anyone builds on the foundation with gold, silver, precious stones, wood, hay, straw—each one's work will become manifest, for the Day will disclose it, because it will be revealed by fire, and the fire will test what sort of work each one has done. If the work that anyone has built on the foundation survives, he will receive a reward. If anyone's work is burned up, he will suffer loss, though he himself will be saved, but only as through fire.

13. What foundation are we building on? What kinds of "building materials" do you think might be straw? What might be gold or silver?

_____

_____

_____

14. Why do you think not all work we do as Christians will last?

_____

_____

_____

In chapter 5, I talk about a simple equation that helps us consider how fruit develops. _____ + TIME = _____ FRUIT. I give a few examples:

Legalism + TIME = *Grouchy* FRUIT
Racial inequality + TIME = *Deadly* FRUIT

15. *What kinds of fruit have you seen develop in your own life, family, or church? What, over time, do you think caused that fruit to develop?*

_____

_____

_____

_____

16. *Consider a few of these equations. What kind of fruit would you predict for each one?*

Fear + TIME = _____ FRUIT
Anger + TIME = _____ FRUIT
Insecurity + TIME = _____ FRUIT
Humility + TIME = _____ FRUIT
Unconditional love + TIME = _____ FRUIT

Time has a way of clarifying things. When we take the long view, we get a glimpse—sometimes a sobering glimpse—of where we might be headed if we stay on the path we're on. Do we want the fruit we're sowing? Or do we want to change what we're cultivating so we reap a sweeter fruit later on?

Inspecting our own fruit is the first step to changing it. In chapter 5, I write:

Don't wait to deal with bad fruit. It won't improve on its own.

The caveat is whether we're able or willing to see clearly enough to evaluate. We lack God's eye for gauging fruit. Our lenses are bent with bias, and our vision is splotched with blind spots. But those who are in Christ aren't left to the strict limitations of our humanness. We have the Lord's indwelling Spirit. Yielding to His authority and affections makes no small difference in our judgment (1 Corinthians 2:12-16). When we look through spiritual eyes, we can see fruit for what it is—we can distinguish between pride and confidence, between self-abasement and humility, between contentiousness and healthy confrontation.

I am desperate for eyes that not only see but perceive (Matthew 13:14).

Read 1 Corinthians 2:12-16.

Now we have received not the spirit of the world, but the Spirit who is from God, that we might understand the things freely given us by God. And we impart this in words not taught by human wisdom but taught by the Spirit, interpreting spiritual truths to those who are spiritual.

The natural person does not accept the things of the Spirit of God, for they are folly to him, and he is not able to understand them because they are spiritually discerned. The spiritual person judges all things, but is himself to be judged by no one. "For who has understood the mind of the Lord so as to instruct him?" But we have the mind of Christ.

17. What does it mean to have spiritual discernment? How does having the Spirit of God help us understand the things of God?

_____

_____

_____

_____

18. How can we grow in discernment?

_____

_____

_____

_____

Inspecting our own fruit with spiritual discernment means we won't always like what we see. Some of our fruit is ripe and lovely, while other fruit is rotten and filled with bugs. Our tendency is to pretend the bad fruit isn't there, to try to spray some spiritual air freshener to cover up the odor of spoiled produce. But as I write in chapter 5, "We will always be better off knowing. Delusion never delivers. Denial can't sweeten acrid grapes. But hard work now can produce a different crop next year."

19. *What do you want to be different in your own motivations, attitudes, and actions?*

_____

_____

_____

20. *How can we find the courage to face our own mistakes and bad fruit? How can the idea of inspecting our fruit bring us hope?*

_____

_____

_____

In chapter 5, I write about being in the fog, unable to see the truth about our own fruit or that of a group we're in—and then suddenly the fog lifts and we can see clearly. The bullet points I list offer some principles I've discovered:

- Honest disunity is better than unity in something dishonest.
- Nothing is unforgivable, but some things cannot be excused.
- When extremism exceeds the commands of Christ, it bears poor fruit.

21. *Which of these principles rings most true for you? What is our responsibility when we realize we're a part of a group that is producing bad fruit?*

_____

_____

_____

22. *Have you ever had a "fog clearing" moment, when something that wasn't clear to you before suddenly became very evident? What did you do as a result?*

_____

_____

_____

_____

Read 2 Corinthians 7:8-10.

Even if I made you grieve with my letter, I do not regret it—though I did regret it, for I see that that letter grieved you, though only for a while. As it is, I rejoice, not because you were grieved, but because you were grieved into repenting. For you felt a godly grief, so that you suffered no loss through us. For godly grief produces a repentance that leads to salvation without regret, whereas worldly grief produces death.

23. *What does godly grief produce? What does worldly grief produce?*

_____

_____

_____

_____

24. *Think of an example from your own life or from the lives of others when godly grief over sin led to repentance and change. What happened?*

_____

_____

_____

_____

This is why examining ourselves and our fruit is so powerful. When our inspection reveals good fruit, we can rejoice and be encouraged by the ways we see God working in our lives. And when our inspection reveals bad fruit, the result is not game-ending condemnation. Rather, it's an opportunity to change. Self-evaluation, with God's help, can motivate us to stop some of the behaviors that are unproductive in our lives and turn to habits that are more life giving and fruit producing.

ROCKS

We read earlier about God bringing His vine, Israel, out of Egypt and transplanting it in the Promised Land. In Isaiah 5, we read about all the ways God prepared and tended His vineyard.

> Let me sing for my beloved
>   my love song concerning his vineyard:
> My beloved had a vineyard
>   on a very fertile hill.
> He dug it and cleared it of stones,
>   and planted it with choice vines.
>
> ISAIAH 5:1-2

In chapter 6, I write,

Every element involved in the Beloved's preparation of the vineyard bears witness to the practices of vine growers throughout time, both in the new world and the old. . . .

He chose a fertile spot.
He selected a place on a hill.
He dug it up.
He cleared it out.
He removed the stones.
He planted the vines.

He removed the stones—but not all of them. Because as I discovered from my Italian cab driver, grapes like the rocky soil. Rocks aren't simply the obstacles the vine-dresser has to contend with; they're something the grapes *require* in order to thrive.

When we think about rocks and soil, we might think about the parable of the sower, which Jesus told to illustrate the way different people receive the gospel. In that parable, rocks are not viewed in a positive light.

Read Matthew 13:3-9.

A sower went out to sow. And as he sowed, some seeds fell along the path, and the birds came and devoured them. Other seeds fell on rocky ground, where they did not have much soil, and immediately they sprang up, since they had no depth of soil, but when the sun rose they were scorched. And since they had no root, they withered away. Other seeds fell among thorns, and the thorns grew up and choked them. Other seeds fell on good soil and produced grain, some a hundredfold, some sixty, some thirty. He who has ears, let him hear.

1. What happened to the seed that fell on rocky ground? Why?

_____

_____

_____

_____

But rocky ground with little soil is different from soil with rocks mixed in. And wheat—the crop in the parable—is different from grapes. Grapes need the obstacles of the rocks.

In chapter 7, I quote plant biologist Jamie Goode:

Making the vines struggle generally results in better quality grapes. . . . If you take a grapevine and make its physical requirements for water and nutrients easily accessible, then (somewhat counterintuitively) it will give you poor grapes. . . .

[Give the grapevine] a favourable environment and it will choose to take the vegetative route: that is, it will put its energies into making leaves and shoots. Effectively, it is saying, "This is a fine spot, I'm going to make myself at home here." It won't be too bothered about making grapes.[*]

[*] Jamie Goode, "Struggling Vines Produce Better Wines," Wineanorak.com, http://www.wineanorak.com/struggle.htm.

Easy conditions lead to bad or little fruit. But make life a little difficult for the vine, and it starts to worry about its survival—and produces fruit to make sure it will live on.

2. *How applicable do you think this concept is for people? In what ways can difficult situations encourage us to produce fruit? How can easy conditions hinder our fruitfulness?*

_____

_____

_____

_____

3. *A vine in comfortable circumstances produces leaves instead of grapes. What might be the human equivalent of producing leaves? What becomes our main motivation when we are living an easy life?*

_____

_____

_____

_____

There's a built-in tension here, isn't there? Rocky soil can help us grow—but too many rocks will keep us from taking good root and cause us to wilt.

In chapter 7, I write,

The landowner looking for the perfect place to plant his choice vine does precisely what the Beloved did in Isaiah 5. He looked for a great spot in a decent climate with generous access to sun, an aspect that could soak in water but also drain it, and the right amount of rocks to make things just challenging enough for his vines to be a little uncomfortable.

The Beloved in Isaiah's song took the shovel and broke up the field to loosen and aerate the soil, but He also performed the task of turning up stones that couldn't be seen from the surface. In doing so, He could survey His ratio of soil to rocks and start sorting.

4. *What are some things God has given you to thrive as a vine—the right climate, sun, water, soil? What are some of the rocks that remain that make life just challenging enough that you stay turned toward God?*

_____

_____

_____

_____

As I write in chapter 7, "In the hands of an able Vinedresser, rocks aren't just something to stub our toe on. They're the very catalysts for our growth. Still, from where we sit, even on this side of the Cross, where death gives way to life, sometimes what God has done for us can feel, instead, like something He has done to us." Read Romans 5:2-5.

We rejoice in hope of the glory of God. Not only that, but we rejoice in our sufferings, knowing that suffering produces endurance, and endurance produces character, and character produces hope, and hope does not put us to shame, because God's love has been poured into our hearts through the Holy Spirit who has been given to us.

5. *According to this passage, why can we rejoice in our sufferings? What do they produce in us?*

_____

_____

_____

_____

In what ways are you struggling with this idea of challenges being a catalyst for growth? It's okay to be honest with yourself and others if you just can't see any good coming out of some of the things you or your family members are facing right now. If that's your situation, ask others in your group to pray that God would comfort you, make His presence known to you, and give you a glimpse of how this difficult situation might be growing you.

The reality is that we all deal with rocks. And some of them seem so big that despite our best efforts to get rid of them, we wonder if they are a reflection of our own failure. In chapter 7, I write,

> With a sketchy background like mine, the simplest explanation [for my continued struggles] is that I sinned so grievously and made so many foolish choices, I sabotaged the rest of my life beyond recovery. But that doesn't sound much like the gospel of Jesus, does it? "You're completely forgiven, slate wiped clean, but, wow, there's nothing I can do about this mess you made."

6. *Do you sometimes believe this lie about God—that there's nothing He can do about your mistakes? If so, how does this belief affect your perception of Him and your ability to trust Him?*

_____

_____

_____

_____

Read Ephesians 3:20 and Romans 8:28.

Now to him who is able to do far more abundantly than all that we ask or think, according to the power at work within us, to him be glory in the church and in Christ Jesus throughout all generations, forever and ever. Amen.

We know that in all things God works for the good of those who love him, who have been called according to his purpose. (NIV)

7. *How do these verses counteract the lie that our mistakes are too big for God to fix? How can they encourage us to trust His ability to use the rocks in our lives for good?*

_____

_____

_____

_____

A big part of trusting God to use our struggles is knowing who He is and trusting His character. Read Psalm 103:10-14.

> He does not deal with us according to our sins,
>   nor repay us according to our iniquities.
> For as high as the heavens are above the earth,
>   so great is his steadfast love toward those
>   who fear him;
> as far as the east is from the west,
>   so far does he remove our transgressions
>   from us.
> As a father shows compassion to his children,
>   so the LORD shows compassion to those
>   who fear him.
> For he knows our frame;
>   he remembers that we are dust.

8. *List some of the ways God treats us, according to this passage.*

_____

_____

_____

_____

9. *How can we interpret our struggles through the lens of this truth? How could this help us react to our rocks with faith instead of doubt?*

_____

_____

_____

_____

Read Isaiah 46:9-10.

Remember the former things of old;
for I am God, and there is no other;
   I am God, and there is none like me,
declaring the end from the beginning
   and from ancient times things not yet done,
saying, "My counsel shall stand,
   and I will accomplish all my purpose."

10. *How do these verses underscore God's sovereignty and omniscience?*

_____

_____

_____

_____

11. *How do these qualities encourage us as we look at our own struggles—the rocks that remain in our soil?*

_____

_____

_____

_____

Here's the other thing about rocks: it's easy to look at other people's fields, trying to make sure their soil is just as rocky as our own. So much of our struggle in dealing with rocks involves our expectations and the way we compare ourselves with others.

Read John 21:17-23.

Jesus said to him, "Feed my sheep. Truly, truly, I say to you, when you were young, you used to dress yourself and walk wherever you wanted, but when you are old, you will stretch out your hands, and another will dress you and carry you where you do not want to go." (This he said to show by what kind of death he was to glorify God.) And after saying this he said to him, "Follow me." Peter turned and saw the disciple whom Jesus loved following them, the one who also had leaned back against him during the supper and had said, "Lord, who is it that is going to betray you?" When Peter saw him, he said to Jesus, "Lord, what about this man?" Jesus said to him, "If it is my will that he remain until I come, what is that to you? You follow me!" So the saying spread abroad among the brothers that this disciple was not to die; yet Jesus did not say to him that he was not to die, but, "If it is my will that he remain until I come, what is that to you?"

12. *What is Peter's response to Jesus telling him how he would one day die? Can you relate to Peter's reaction?*

_____

_____

_____

_____

This exchange takes place after Jesus' resurrection. The Gospels tell us that Jesus had already appeared to the disciples at least once, but in this passage, He appears to them on the beach after they've been fishing all night. This may have been the first extended conversation Peter had with Jesus since before His death—and since he denied even knowing Jesus (three times, no less!). Here Jesus reinstates Peter, telling him to "feed [His] sheep," and then He suggests that Peter will one day be martyred as a result. Perhaps it's no surprise that Peter responds to this difficult news by looking at others—specifically John. "What about him?"

13. *How does Jesus respond to Peter's question? What does He say Peter needs to do?*

_____

_____

_____

_____

14. *Based on this passage, what is the best antidote to comparison? What are some practical steps we can take to focus on following Jesus?*

In chapter 7, I write,

I can't explain why the soil of some tremendously fruitful lives doesn't seem to be as stone prone, but I'm pretty sure Jesus thinks that's none of my business.

Our part is to follow Jesus. He knows what He's doing with you. No one's loved more than you. No one's a bigger priority than you. No one else is so high on His list of favorites that your contribution to the body of Christ is drowned out or diminished.

In fact, God doesn't play favorites.

15. *What do you think it means that God doesn't have favorites? How can we believe this about God when we're facing difficult circumstances?*

_____

_____

_____

_____

Read Hebrews 12:1-2.

Since we are surrounded by so great a cloud of witnesses, let us also lay aside every weight, and sin which clings so closely, and let us run with endurance the race that is set before us, looking to Jesus, the founder and perfecter of our faith, who for the joy that was set before him endured the cross, despising the shame, and is seated at the right hand of the throne of God.

16. *According to this passage, what helps us run the race before us?*

_____

_____

_____

_____

17. *Some Bible versions translate the beginning of verse 2 as "fixing our eyes on Jesus." How does keeping our eyes on Him rather than on our challenges renew our perspective and increase our endurance?*

_____

_____

_____

_____

— *Wrapping Up* —

In chapter 7, I talk about some of the challenges that remain in my life. I hope this will encourage you that struggles are a reality for many—perhaps most—people. If you are facing something difficult right now, you're not alone. Life is rocky, hard, and rarely smooth. And yet we can hold on to this truth: the rocks do not prevent fruitfulness. In fact, sometimes they *enable* fruitfulness.

Sixty years in, I have a feeling the rocky soil in the life of the Jesus follower is not so much about failure as it is about fruitfulness. I think one of these days, after we've seen Christ face-to-face, He may get around to saying something like, "Remember all those hard things I grew you through? I did you a favor. You can thank Me now." And I bet we will, and on that side of things, I bet we'll mean it. . . .

The favor is dependency. We who have never stopped wanting Jesus have likely never stopped needing Jesus. And if our passion waned for a brief while, we were always only one crisis from the next revival.

It may be hard for us to imagine right now, but there will come a day when we will fully understand the way these stones have deepened our faith, caused us to rely more wholly on God, and helped us bear a great crop of juicy, ripe fruit.

— Deepening Our Roots —

On your own this week, try one or two of these activities:

- Take some time to review the list of questions on page 29. Ask God to help you accurately evaluate the fruit in your life, remembering that He is on your side.
- Review the "Time + _____" equations on page 31. In a journal, write about one kind of fruit that has developed in your life over the years. What new ingredient would you like to add to time to develop different fruit in the future?
- Listen to a song or hymn that encourages you to see your challenges as opportunities to trust God.
- Reread Romans 5:1-5 every day this week as an encouragement that God is using the rocks in your life to develop your character and give you hope.

The Vine

I am the vine; you are the branches.
Whoever abides in me and I in him,
he it is that bears much fruit.

JOHN 15:5

GROUP GATHERING

Discussion: As a group, discuss your answers to the selected questions in the previous "On Your Own" section based on part 2, "The Vinedresser."

Watch session 3 of the DVD.

— *Listening Guide* —

1. What ideas or phrases in the DVD segment caught your attention?

_____

_____

_____

_____

2. *What do you think of when you hear the term* abide? *What does abiding in Christ mean to you?*

_____

_____

_____

_____

3. *In his book* The Confessions, *early Christian theologian Augustine says, "How sweet all at once it was for me to be rid of those fruitless joys which I had once feared to lose . . . ! You drove them from me, you who are the true, the sovereign joy. You drove them from me and took their place, you who are sweeter than all pleasure, though not to flesh and blood, you who outshine all light, yet are hidden deeper than any secret in our hearts, you who surpass all honor, though not in the eyes of men who see all honor in themselves . . . O Lord my God, my Light, my Wealth, and my Salvation." What is your reaction to this quote? In what ways does it ring true to your own experiences or longings?*

_____

_____

_____

_____

_____

_____

_____

— *Prayer* —

Take some time to share concerns with your group and pray together. Ask God to help you learn more fully this week what it means to abide in Him, acknowledging your dependence on Him and enjoying His presence. Pray that He would continue to train you in the way of the Cross as you follow Him.

+ + +

ON YOUR OWN

During the week, read part 3 ("The Vine") of *Chasing Vines*. Then proceed with "A Word from Beth" and this week's homework. You're doing such a great job! Keep going! Immense fruitfulness is ahead.

— *A Word from Beth* —

In the third part of *Chasing Vines*, "The Vine," we consider what it means to abide in the true Vine, Jesus, letting everything else fade away until we're clinging to Christ alone. As branches of the Vine, we are fully dependent on Him for life, support, and fruitfulness.

I write in chapter 8,

If you're in Christ, He is your true Vine, whether you realize it or not. But a whole new way of flourishing begins when you know it. When you count on it. When you live like it. When you let go of the vines you thought were giving you life.

Together, let's learn to depend on Him and begin to walk the way of the Cross.

— *Planting the Seed* —

ABIDE

The word *abide* seems passive to many of us. It conveys waiting, resting, being still. Simple—and yet it's the key to living in Christ. It's also the centerpiece of Jesus' words in John 15.

In chapter 9, I write,

In one sense, abiding sounds like the easiest command for a Jesus-follower to undertake. It means resting in the One who is stronger than we are, wiser than we are, and more powerful than we are—and who loves us and defends us. But for most of us, the not-doing is infinitely more difficult than the doing. Give us a to-do list or a deadline or an assignment, but for the love, please don't ask us to let go and be still.

1. Why is doing *often so much easier for us than* being*? What might God be able to accomplish in us when we're resting in Him that He can't when we're busy doing things on our own?*

_____

_____

_____

_____

Read Psalm 46:10-11.

"Be still, and know that I am God.
    I will be exalted among the nations,
    I will be exalted in the earth!"

The LORD of hosts is with us;
    the God of Jacob is our fortress.

2. In this psalm, what does being still allow us to focus on?

_____

_____

_____

_____

In earlier chapters we talked about the vine representing Israel and being transplanted from Egypt to the Promised Land. But then Jesus changed all that by saying that *He* is the true vine. With Jesus on the scene, God was doing a new thing. This is a good time to nail down an important principle of abiding. It doesn't mean we're immobilized. That's the beauty of Christ turning this metaphor on its head. The vine, which was once the land, has now been supplanted by Christ. That means we no longer abide in a place but in a person. We reside in Jesus. When He moves, we move. When He stays, we stay.

3. *What is significant about abiding in a person rather than in a place?*

_____

_____

_____

_____

In chapter 9, I recount the story of a woman who spent long years in prison for a crime she didn't commit before eventually being exonerated. She spent her time in prison studying God's Word—and she found true liberty in Christ. She said, "I'm totally free in Jesus! Even in prison, I was free."

Whether she was behind bars on a paper-thin mattress or running through a field of sunflowers, that girl was free. She'd found joy inside and joy outside because Jesus Himself was her joy, and no one could take Him away.

4. *What holds us back from experiencing true freedom in Christ? How can abiding in Jesus release us from other things that might have a hold on us?*

_____

_____

_____

_____

Abiding is inextricably connected with fruitfulness. Read John 15:4-5.

Abide in me, and I in you. As the branch cannot bear fruit by itself, unless it abides in the vine, neither can you, unless you abide in me. I am the vine;

you are the branches. Whoever abides in me and I in him, he it is that bears much fruit, for apart from me you can do nothing.

If we're honest, we've all had times when we were not remotely abiding in Jesus and yet we seemed to get a lot done—even a lot of good things. But what we can accomplish when we're abiding in Christ is something else entirely.

The context of John 15:5 communicates something closer to this: "Apart from Me you can do nothing you couldn't do anyway." Said another way, "Apart from me, you can do nothing only I can do." John 15 is about living a naturally unexplainable life. It's about doing what we can't do on our own and becoming who we can't be on our own.

5. *When have you seen evidence of Jesus working through you to do something you couldn't do on your own? (Forgiving someone who hurt you? Reaching out to someone who is struggling or lonely? Having the energy or focus to begin a ministry or serve patiently behind the scenes?) When have you seen Jesus working through someone else to do what would have seemed impossible on their own?*

_____

_____

_____

_____

6. *How can this connection between fruitfulness and abiding release us from thinking we can win God's approval by doing more for Him?*

_____

_____

_____

_____

Abiding in Christ brings increased fruitfulness, but abiding isn't just about being productive. It's also relational. At its core, it involves getting to know Christ better and better. And that's a reward in and of itself.

The concept of abiding—spending time with God for His delight and ours—sets

Christianity apart from other religions and worldviews. Yet sometimes we are afraid or unwilling to take this radical approach. Sometimes we would rather do things in what seems like an easier way.

In chapter 8, I write,

Could it be that what God loves most about His relationship with us is precisely what we do not love about it? He loves to be with us, sit with us, and walk with us. He loves to be in our company, as hard as that is for us to fathom, and to be company to us. He didn't need disciples. He could have accomplished every task He desired without them. He chose the disciples to have "part with [Him]" (John 13:8), to partner with Him (2 Corinthians 6:1).

God doesn't need us, either. He could accomplish all He wills from the throne of heaven. He *wants* us with Him. He longs for a relationship with us. While God desires the relational, however, we humans tend toward the transactional. "Lord, just tell me what to do and give me the power to perform it. Then let me do it." We say to the Alpha and Omega, "Give me the plan from A to Z, and leave it to me."

We forget that He came to be Immanuel, God with us.

7. *What can be frightening or unnerving about God being Immanuel, God with us? Why do we tend to favor a transactional relationship with God instead of one based on love and delight?*

Read John 15:15 and 1 John 3:1.

No longer do I call you servants, for the servant does not know what his master is doing; but I have called you friends, for all that I have heard from my Father I have made known to you.

See what kind of love the Father has given to us, that we should be called children of God; and so we are.

8. *What do these verses show us about the kind of relationship God desires to have with us?*

_____

_____

_____

So many other faiths are built on transactions. In the pagan world at the time the Israelites were transplanted to the Promised Land, the religious climate was all about giving to get. People who offered a sacrifice would expect a tangible blessing in return. And once they gave their sacrifice and received their blessing, they could live on their own terms until the next time they needed something.

Isn't that what we sometimes want too? We want to be self-sufficient, as if we can manage just fine on our own, and we view needing God as a moment of weakness and something to be minimized. Yet God wants us to recognize our dependence on Him each second of the day—and to know that this is actually a good thing. He made us to need Him, and He wants to be a part of our every breath, our every moment. He has more to give us than the little things we ask for; He gives us Himself.

Read 2 Corinthians 3:16-18.

When one turns to the Lord, the veil is removed. Now the Lord is the Spirit, and where the Spirit of the Lord is, there is freedom. And we all, with unveiled face, beholding the glory of the Lord, are being transformed into the same image from one degree of glory to another. For this comes from the Lord who is the Spirit.

9. *What are the results of seeing the Lord more clearly? How are we being transformed as we experience more of God?*

_____

_____

_____

Part of abiding with God means that we rely on Him moment by moment for His direction.

In chapter 8, I write,

From the very beginning, God geared the faith walk to be relational, not informational. The latter was always intended for the sake of the former.

We want to leap with God; He wants to walk with us. Walking transpires step by step. It demands patience. Pacing. God's directional leading for our personal lives often unfurls in bits of light between shadows. He says His word is a lamp to our feet, which offers us the assurance of arm's length direction when He says, "Go."

10. *Leaders, teachers, and parents guide with the expectation that eventually they will no longer be needed. How does God's way of guiding us differ?*

_____

_____

_____

_____

11. *When have you experienced this sense of God showing you only the next step instead of the whole plan?*

_____

_____

_____

_____

Read Genesis 12:1 and Exodus 4:12.

The LORD said to Abram, "Go from your country and your kindred and your father's house to the land that I will show you."

[God said to Moses,] "Now therefore go, and I will be with your mouth and teach you what you shall speak."

12. *Why do you think God didn't give Abram and Moses a full set of instructions at the beginning of their stories? How did their situations require continued dependence on God?*

_____

_____

_____

_____

Have you ever read a novel or seen a movie where the main characters set off on a quest with a set of instructions? For some reason the characters never have the instructions in writing, so they must review them mentally or verbally every day. Inevitably, they begin to forget the details, and sooner or later they miss something important that changes the shape or scope of the quest. I'm so glad that's not the way God leads us. He doesn't give us the directions from start to finish and then step back to evaluate just how well we'll carry them out. No, He walks alongside us, illuminating each step and encouraging us to stay on the right path. Psalm 23 tells us that He leads us "in paths of righteousness" as a shepherd.

In chapter 9, I write,

Being a branch to the true Vine means living with Christ, breathing with Christ, doing day-to-day life with Christ. It's the ongoing awareness of His presence, even when there's no feeling of His presence. Our lives become witness to His with-ness.

13. *How can we become more aware of God's presence, His "with-ness"? What practical steps can you take to remember that you are constantly connected with Him?*

_____

_____

_____

_____

In chapter 9, I quote Dr. Gary M. Burge as he talks about living in true connection with Christ: "What are the outcomes of this sort of life? The fruit Jesus expects from the branches is first and foremost love." Abiding in Jesus—knowing Him better and being connected with Him—leads to becoming more like Him. And that means abounding in love.

14. *Is it a paradigm shift for you to think about loving God and loving others as a kind of fruit? How does this differ from what we often think of as fruitfulness?*

_____

_____

_____

_____

Read 1 John 4:7-12.

Beloved, let us love one another, for love is from God, and whoever loves has been born of God and knows God. Anyone who does not love does not know God, because God is love. In this the love of God was made manifest among us, that God sent his only Son into the world, so that we might live through him. In this is love, not that we have loved God but that he loved us and sent his Son to be the propitiation for our sins. Beloved, if God so loved us, we also ought to love one another. No one has ever seen God; if we love one another, God abides in us and his love is perfected in us.

15. *What does this passage tell us about the connection between God's love for us and our love for others? How does focusing on God and who He is help increase our love for others?*

_____

_____

_____

_____

16.Consider how you could better show love to those around you this week.

_____

_____

_____

_____

TRELLIS

I open chapter 11 by writing about a mother who brought her young daughter to a conference to meet me. She introduced her by saying, "She has a background like yours"—which I immediately understood to mean a background of abuse.

> It was one of those moments when you know you'd better choose your words with utmost care. She needed to know that she mattered. That her pain mattered. That there was hope for her. That she wasn't just meant to survive but to thrive.
>
> So I cupped her face in my hands. "Oh, my goodness," I said. "I am so sorry. But do you know what that means?"
>
> She shook her head.
>
> "That means you get to learn how to be strong in Jesus in a way lots of other people won't. You get to learn who you are in Him and how precious you are to Him, because people like you and me must, in order to have healthy, happy hearts. We get to know Jesus the way some people never bother knowing Him. Somebody very wrong made us feel really small, but now we get to learn how to stand really, really tall."

1.Has a particular challenge prompted you to know Jesus better? How can devastating circumstances drive us to find our identity in Him and to know His love for us?

_____

_____

_____

_____

The apostle Paul faced some significant challenges. Read 2 Corinthians 12:7-10.

A thorn was given me in the flesh, a messenger of Satan to harass me, to keep me from becoming conceited. Three times I pleaded with the Lord about this, that it should leave me. But he said to me, "My grace is sufficient for you, for my power is made perfect in weakness." Therefore I will boast all the more gladly of my weaknesses, so that the power of Christ may rest upon me. For the sake of Christ, then, I am content with weaknesses, insults, hardships, persecutions, and calamities. For when I am weak, then I am strong.

2. Why could Paul boast in his weaknesses?

_____

_____

_____

_____

3. What does it mean for us to be content with our own failings and the hardships we encounter? How can we be strong in the midst of our weaknesses?

_____

_____

_____

_____

God doesn't promise that we'll avoid pain because we follow Him. He doesn't promise that we'll escape trauma or abuse or divorce or illness or pain or death. But He does promise a way up. A way through. Or a way out. If we offer our pain to Him, in all its horror and ugliness, and receive His offer to redeem what has happened to us, He will bring fruit from it.

Who but God could do this? Who else could bring hope and life out of the worst things in our lives? Only the One whose sovereignty extends as far as His love. Only the One who has walked the way of the Cross.

Jesus calls us to follow Him in the way of the Cross, but that way doesn't come naturally to us. That's why God trains us in it.

In chapter 11, I describe the way the vinedresser uses stakes or a trellis to support the growing vines.

Stroll through the rows of any functioning vineyard, and you'll notice that the posture of a grapevine is a direct reflection of the apparatus it's attached to. Simply put, the way it's trained is the way it will grow. The apparatus may be anything from a single grape stake to an elaborate archway trellis, but whatever form it takes, the growing vine needs adequate support. The branches cannot carry the weight of immense fruitfulness on their own. . . .

If the vinedresser doesn't take over, the branches will. And if the branches take over, the vine's productivity suffers and the delectable taste of the fruit goes untapped.

4. *If we apply this to ourselves as branches of the vine, what do you think it means for us to grow in the way we are trained?*

_____

_____

_____

_____

If we grow the way we are trained—if we grow in the shape of the stake or trellis to which we as branches are tied—then it's imperative that we're staked to the right thing. And that thing is the Cross of Christ. No matter what others stake their lives on. No matter if the world thinks it's a waste of time. No matter if some days we even doubt its truth.

Read 1 Corinthians 1:18-19.

The message of the cross is foolishness to those who are perishing, but to us who are being saved it is the power of God. For it is written:

"I will destroy the wisdom of the wise;
the intelligence of the intelligent I will frustrate." (NIV)

5. *Why does the message of the Cross seem foolish to those who are perishing? How is it the "power of God" in our lives?*

_____

_____

_____

_____

6. *How can this truth encourage us when we doubt?*

_____

_____

_____

_____

Learning the way of the Cross is not easy. It involves sacrifice, self-denial, and long-term thinking.

In chapter 11, I write,

Yet it remains our only means of finding true life—not just after we shed these temporal bodies, but right here, right now. On this very earth, in this very era, on the very block where we live.

The way of the Cross teaches sacrificial love to otherwise self-seeking, self-absorbed, self-exalting creatures who can never seem to get enough of themselves to satisfy themselves. . . . The way of the Cross is painful, to be sure, but it is also a peculiar relief. Over the long haul, the weight of an unchecked human ego becomes a heavier load to bear than a cross.

7. *Take a moment to reflect on our culture. Where do you see evidence that an "unchecked human ego" is a heavy burden to carry?*

_____

_____

_____

_____

_____

8. *What is the end result of centering our lives on ourselves? Why are we never satisfied when we are absorbed in ourselves?*

_____

_____

_____

_____

_____

Read Philippians 2:3-11.

Do nothing from selfish ambition or conceit, but in humility count others more significant than yourselves. Let each of you look not only to his own interests, but also to the interests of others. Have this mind among yourselves, which is yours in Christ Jesus, who, though he was in the form of God, did not count equality with God a thing to be grasped, but emptied himself, by taking the form of a servant, being born in the likeness of men. And being found in human form, he humbled himself by becoming obedient to the point of death, even death on a cross. Therefore God has highly exalted him and bestowed on him the name that is above every name, so that at the name of Jesus every knee should bow, in heaven and on earth and under the earth, and every tongue confess that Jesus Christ is Lord, to the glory of God the Father.

9. *List some characteristics that Paul encourages us to emulate.*

_____

_____

_____

_____

10. *In what specific ways does the character of Christ contrast with our culture's focus on self?*

_____

_____

_____

_____

To follow the way of the Cross, we have to look deeper—and more long term. We have to look past what feels good and entertaining and satisfying right now, and look to the burden those things lead to. We need to embrace what might seem difficult now but will bring great reward later—the reward of God's presence and living our most fulfilled lives.

In chapter 11, I write,

> God knew it would take a cross to crucify us to the world. The death of His Son by countless other means would bear less stigma, less ridicule, less mess. God chose a means by which we could not have our pride and our salvation too. . . .
>
> The training system of the Cross ties the branches of the true Vine to humility. The prouder we are, the further we move away from it.

11. *Why do you think there is an inverse relationship between pride and the Cross? What happens if we try to hang on to both our pride and our salvation?*

_____

_____

_____

_____

12. What are some ways that clinging to Christ and His Cross develop humility in us? What fruit might humility produce?

_____

_____

_____

_____

Read 1 Corinthians 1:26-31.

Consider your calling, brothers: not many of you were wise according to worldly standards, not many were powerful, not many were of noble birth. But God chose what is foolish in the world to shame the wise; God chose what is weak in the world to shame the strong; God chose what is low and despised in the world, even things that are not, to bring to nothing things that are, so that no human being might boast in the presence of God. And because of him you are in Christ Jesus, who became to us wisdom from God, righteousness and sanctification and redemption, so that, as it is written, "Let the one who boasts, boast in the Lord."

13. According to this passage, why did God choose the foolish and low and weak things of the world?

_____

_____

_____

_____

14. What do you think it means to "boast in the Lord"? How does boasting in the Lord produce humility in us?

_____

_____

_____

_____

15. *When have you found you needed to put aside pride to draw close to Christ? In practical terms, what does humility look like?*

_____

_____

_____

_____

The way of the Cross leads us to humility. And in our humility, it leads us on to forgiveness.

Without a trellis, the vine would fold in on itself, remaining stuck at ground level. Without a trellis, the branches would never reach their heads up to the sun. And so the trellis of the Cross trains us in the way of forgiveness (Luke 23:33-35). It lifts our heads from the dirt and sludge and raises our faces to the Son—the same Son who prayed from the Cross, "Father, forgive them, for they know not what they do" while strangers gawked at Him, rulers scoffed at Him, and soldiers cast lots for His clothing. An unforgiving Christian is the embodiment of an oxymoron. God help me, I've been one. I suppose we all have. Life hands us plenty of opportunities to practice the dichotomy.

We all have people we struggle to forgive, often because the hurts are too deep and the perpetrator's repentance is too shallow. This may be too sensitive to discuss as a group, so I'll encourage you to think about it individually later. For now, let's acknowledge that all of us are wounded. Keep that in mind as we discuss forgiveness.

I've become increasingly convinced that those we need to forgive most often grasp the least how much they've hurt us. If they understood and took responsibility, it wouldn't have taken the Cross to forgive them. It could have just happened over coffee.

The way of the Cross is forgiveness—raw and bloody and gasping for air. It seldom follows earnest shouts of "I'm sorry!" More likely, it's surrounded by the sounds of "Crucify him!"

16. *Does this perspective on forgiveness resonate with you? Why do you think it's most important for us to forgive those who least understand what they have done to us? What changes for us after we forgive them?*

_____

_____

_____

_____

17. *How do we begin to forgive those who have wronged us? What steps can we take?*

_____

_____

_____

_____

Read Matthew 18:23-33.

Therefore the kingdom of heaven may be compared to a king who wished to settle accounts with his servants. When he began to settle, one was brought to him who owed him ten thousand talents. And since he could not pay, his master ordered him to be sold, with his wife and children and all that he had, and payment to be made. So the servant fell on his knees, imploring him, "Have patience with me, and I will pay you everything." And out of pity for him, the master of that servant released him and forgave him the debt. But when that same servant went out, he found one of his fellow servants who owed him a hundred denarii, and seizing him, he began to choke him, saying, "Pay what you owe." So his fellow servant fell down and pleaded with him, "Have patience with me, and I will pay you." He refused and went and put him in prison until he should pay the debt. When his fellow servants saw what had taken place, they were greatly distressed, and they went and reported to their master all that had taken place. Then his master summoned him and said to him, "You wicked servant! I forgave you all that debt because you pleaded with me. And should not you have had mercy on your fellow servant, as I had mercy on you?"

18. *Who represents God in this parable? Who represents people who don't forgive those who have hurt them?*

_____

_____

_____

_____

19. *Why were the fellow servants so distressed by the unforgiving servant's actions? Why does his hard-heartedness toward the man who owed him money seem so unthinkable?*

_____

_____

_____

_____

20. *What is the takeaway for us? Why should we forgive those who have wronged us?*

_____

_____

_____

_____

_____

This parable can be hard to read if our wounds are deep. We may feel that what the other person did to us was far more significant than any way we could have sinned against God. Hear me when I say that I'm the last person to minimize your pain or excuse someone else's sin against you. And yet when we take a clear look at ourselves and a clear look at God, we begin to see the depth of our own selfishness and pride and wrong choices—and the depth of God's holiness.

In chapter 11, I talk about a woman I met who was unable to accept God's forgiveness. She felt so unclean she couldn't let herself bathe. Most of us don't experience shame to this extent, but we all understand the gut-wrenching, soul-twisting reality of something we've done that we desperately wish we could undo. Maybe those around us have offered their forgiveness, and yet we hold tightly to our sin, sure that nobody can actually cleanse us from it. We've made a mistake, and now we're stuck with it forever. Even God can't forgive *that*.

Read Ephesians 2:4-9.

Because of his great love for us, God, who is rich in mercy, made us alive with Christ even when we were dead in transgressions—it is by grace you have been saved. And God raised us up with Christ and seated us with him in the heavenly realms in Christ Jesus, in order that in the coming ages he might show the incomparable riches of his grace, expressed in his kindness to us in Christ Jesus. For it is by grace you have been saved, through faith—and this is not from yourselves, it is the gift of God—not by works, so that no one can boast. (NIV)

21. What words in this passage reflect the abundance of God's grace?

_____

_____

_____

_____

22. Reflect on the contrast between being "dead in transgressions" and "alive with Christ." What relief do we find in the fact that this is a gift of God rather than something we deserve or can achieve on our own?

_____

_____

_____

_____

Read Psalm 103:8-12.

The LORD is merciful and gracious,
  slow to anger and abounding in steadfast love.
He will not always chide,
  nor will he keep his anger forever.
He does not deal with us according to our sins,
  nor repay us according to our iniquities.
For as high as the heavens are above the earth,
  so great is his steadfast love toward those who fear him;
as far as the east is from the west,
  so far does he remove our transgressions from us.

23. *What visual images does the psalmist use to show how God has removed our sins?*

_____

_____

_____

_____

24. *What adjectives are used to describe God?*

_____

_____

_____

_____

25. *Can you think of a time when someone forgave you for a wrong you had done? How did you respond? How did it change your relationship going forward?*

_____

_____

_____

_____

Accepting God's forgiveness frees us from shame, from wallowing in guilt, from our fear that someone might discover the truth about us. We can walk freely in the grace of God. And that freedom—which stems from an awareness of how much we have been forgiven—bears great fruit in our lives.

— *Wrapping Up* —

The way of the Cross demands much from us but gives us even more. It produces beautiful qualities in us—love, dependence on God, humility, forgiveness. And it brings us closer to Jesus, allowing us to abide in Him.

We are being trained and taught by our loving Father to live in Him and with Him in every moment. This is our training. Our trellis. When the branch abides in the Vine, forgiveness is wholly unobstructed. It flows freely, both vertically and horizontally.

Welcome, one and all, to the way of the Cross.

— *Deepening Our Roots* —

On your own this week, try one or two of these activities:

- Think about these paraphrases of John 15:5: "Apart from Me you can do nothing you couldn't do anyway." "Apart from Me, you can do nothing only I can do." In a journal, reflect on what fruit in your life is rooted in your own gifts and abilities. Where do you see God helping you do what you couldn't do on your own?
- Add a regular alarm to your phone as a reminder of God's constant presence with you and your dependence on Him. Or add notes to your bathroom mirror, kitchen counter, car dashboard, or anywhere else you will see them.
- Think of a tangible way to share God's love with someone this week— perhaps by writing a note, inviting the person over for coffee, bringing a meal, or sharing an encouraging Scripture passage.
- Reread the parable of the unforgiving servant (Matthew 18:23-33) and Ephesians 2:4-8. Meditate on both passages. Spend some time in prayer, thanking God for His forgiveness and asking Him to show you if there's anyone you need to forgive—including yourself.

The Fruit

Unless a grain of wheat falls into the earth and dies, it remains alone;
but if it dies, it bears much fruit.

JOHN 12:24

GROUP GATHERING

Discussion: As a group, discuss your answers to the selected questions in the previous "On Your Own" section based on part 3, "The Vine."

Watch session 4 of the DVD.

— Listening Guide —

1. What ideas or phrases in the DVD segment caught your attention?

_____

_____

_____

_____

2. Every divine _____ in a human life entails _____ and _____.

— *Prayer* —

Take some time to share concerns with your group and pray together. Ask God to help you grasp the truth and scope of His love, and to make that knowledge your most closely held belief. Pray that God would give you the ability to see the devil's attacks for what they are and resist them, instead clinging to the good news of who God is and what He has done for us.

✦ ✦ ✦

ON YOUR OWN

During the week, read part 4 ("The Fruit") of *Chasing Vines*. Then proceed with "A Word from Beth" and this week's homework. I'm praying for you, and I'm so honored to take this journey with you.

— *A Word from Beth* —

At the beginning of chapter 13, I talk about the "phone call that would forever divide the timeline of the Moore family into two distinct periods: before and after." Maybe you've experienced something similar, where your loss is so great that you can't imagine life ever being the same.

And it's true. Life never goes back to the way it was. And yet we do heal—slowly, gradually, imperfectly.

In chapter 13, I write,

I think most of the time when light comes back into our lives, it works more like a dimmer than a switch. There wasn't one particular moment the light switch flipped. A sliver of light would slip in, and we'd huddle close and try to sun our faces before the darkness descended again—and it always did.

Our family's grief, as it is for most people, came in gradations of black to gray. Life never was the same again—it can't be after that kind of loss. But by God's grace, the sun did come out from behind the clouds again, and often enough to warm the blood in our cold bones.

What gets us through a crisis like this? How do we stop looking backward and begin to look ahead? The answer lies in what our roots grow down into.

Planting the Seed

ROOTS

If death is the heaviest loss for us as individuals, it's difficult to think of a more devastating situation on a community level than the seeming impending destruction of a country. That's what Judah was facing when the great Assyrian empire began to move against them.

By this time in the history of God's people, the country had been split into two kingdoms—Israel in the north and Judah in the south. Israel, which had had a series of terrible kings who actively pursued idol worship, had already fallen to Assyria, and it wasn't pretty. The Assyrian king had resettled some of his own people in Israel, taking over their lands and cities. Many of the Israelites had been forced to make the long trek to Assyria, knowing they would live out the rest of their lives far from home in one of the cruelest pagan cultures in history. And now the people of Judah wondered if they would suffer the same fate. The same people who had been given the Promised Land—who had been the vine God transplanted from Egypt into the land He had prepared for them—now wondered if they would be uprooted.

After the Assyrian general publicly threatened Judah and insulted the Lord, the prophet Isaiah told what would ultimately happen to Assyria. Read his assurances to King Hezekiah in Isaiah 37:30-35.

This shall be the sign for you: this year you shall eat what grows of itself, and in the second year what springs from that. Then in the third year sow and reap, and plant vineyards, and eat their fruit. And the surviving remnant of the house of Judah shall again take root downward and bear fruit upward. For out of Jerusalem shall go a remnant, and out of Mount Zion a band of survivors. The zeal of the LORD of hosts will do this.

Therefore thus says the LORD concerning the king of Assyria: He shall not come into this city or shoot an arrow there or come before it with a shield or cast up a siege mound against it. By the way that he came, by the same he shall return, and he shall not come into this city, declares the LORD. For I will defend this city to save it, for my own sake and for the sake of my servant David."

1. List some of the things God will bring about, according to verses 33-35.

_____

_____

_____

_____

While some of the people were safe behind the walls of the cities, their crops and livestock were not. The Assyrian army would have eaten any crops that were ripe and destroyed the rest. The country had suffered devastating loss—and yet God, through Isaiah, spoke hope.

2. What hope for the future do we see in verses 30-32?

_____

_____

_____

_____

Although this situation wouldn't be erased, God was assuring the people that it would pass. And they would find His goodness and faithfulness on the other side, because He would still be with them. In chapter 13, I write:

When we're going through a difficult season, wouldn't the best news of all be that life would simply go back to normal someday? When the framework of our daily existence gets completely dismantled and the landscape around us grows increasingly unrecognizable, our strongest longing is seldom prosperity. What we yearn for is normalcy. We don't tend to ask for the moon when we've lost all we've known. We just want some semblance of our old lives back.

The hard truth is, there's no real going back. But once we get up again, there can be a going forward. In His faithfulness, God sees to it what we thought was the end isn't the end after all. And eventually, perhaps not terribly long after, we realize we've transitioned into a new normal.

3. *When have you had to face the fact that there would be no returning to "normal life" after a loss or hard thing that changed you? Were you able to find a new normal? What helped you move forward?*

_____

_____

_____

_____

It's human nature to focus on what has changed in our lives and to long for what we once had. But when we're faced with the pain and anxiety of loss and change, perhaps we should fix our minds on what remains the same in our lives. God is constant even when our circumstances are not.

Read Psalm 102:25-28 and Matthew 28:20.

Of old you laid the foundation of the earth,
    and the heavens are the work of your hands.
They will perish, but you will remain;
    they will all wear out like a garment.
You will change them like a robe, and they will
        pass away,
    but you are the same, and your years have no end.
The children of your servants shall dwell secure;
    their offspring shall be established before you.

[Jesus said,] "Behold, I am with you always, to the end of the age."

4. What do these verses communicate about God's unchanging nature and His relationship with us? How can this knowledge comfort us when we go through loss and change?

_____

_____

_____

_____

God's people would plant and harvest again—because He had not changed, even though their circumstances had. And God's constant, miraculous work in our lives means that even after our lives seem to have been utterly destroyed, God can make them fruitful again. They can still matter.

In chapter 13, I write,

Whether or not our physical surroundings ever again resemble what we once knew, if we have an ounce of breath on the other side, we can bear much fruit again.

Maybe right now that promise doesn't mean a lot. You don't want a remnant; you want all the same people back. And truth be told, you'd prefer them at all their former ages and stages. You don't want to grow something new. You want to return to your old life. You want those exact clusters of grapes, not new ones. You want everything to taste exactly like it once did.

I understand. But in time, finding fruitfulness again will make more difference than you can imagine. If we can't have our treasured yesterday back, at least tomorrow can matter. The wonder of fruit bearing is that something meaningful can come from the meanest of seasons. What we endured matters.

Scripture states this clearly. Read James 1:2-4.

Count it all joy, my brothers, when you meet trials of various kinds, for you know that the testing of your faith produces steadfastness. And let steadfastness have its full effect, that you may be perfect and complete, lacking in nothing.

5. *What do trials produce in us? How do you think this works?*

_____

_____

_____

_____

It's important to note that we can believe our struggles matter without believing those struggles were "worth it." No matter how much good comes from a personal tragedy, we may always wish it hadn't happened. We may praise God for the results without being able to say with confidence that we would do it all again. But fortunately we don't have to decide.

6. *When have you felt burdened by this expectation that you need to make the loss or struggle worth it? Does it help to think only of making it matter?*

_____

_____

_____

_____

In chapter 13, I write,

Yes, Christ can bring fruit from His followers' incalculable suffering. But on this side of eternity, the point isn't making it worth it. It's about making it matter. *Jesus* is worth it. He's worth trusting. He's worth anticipating. He's worth getting out of bed for when you wish you could go to sleep and never wake up. You may have to believe that by faith until faith becomes sight.

Read Matthew 13:44-46.

[Jesus said,] "The kingdom of heaven is like treasure hidden in a field, which a man found and covered up. Then in his joy he goes and sells all that he has and buys that field.

"Again, the kingdom of heaven is like a merchant in search of fine pearls, who, on finding one pearl of great value, went and sold all that he had and bought it."

7. *What prompts the people in the parables to sell all that they had?*

_____

_____

_____

_____

8. *Do we believe that Jesus is this kind of treasure—not just because of what He gives us but because of who He is? How can we remember that He is worth it and that trusting Him brings great treasure?*

_____

_____

_____

_____

Read the apostle Paul's words in Philippians 3:4-11.

If anyone else thinks he has reason for confidence in the flesh, I have more: circumcised on the eighth day, of the people of Israel, of the tribe of Benjamin, a Hebrew of Hebrews; as to the law, a Pharisee; as to zeal, a persecutor of the church; as to righteousness under the law, blameless. But whatever gain I had, I counted as loss for the sake of Christ. Indeed, I count everything as loss because of the surpassing worth of knowing Christ Jesus my Lord. For his sake I have suffered the loss of all things and count them as rubbish, in order that I may gain Christ and be found in him, not having a righteousness of my own that comes from the law, but that which comes through faith in Christ, the righteousness from God that depends on faith—that I may know him and the power of his resurrection, and may share his sufferings, becoming like him in his death, that by any means possible I may attain the resurrection from the dead.

9. *What things does Paul categorize as "loss" or "rubbish"? What does he say has "surpassing worth"? What is Paul's ultimate hope?*

_____

_____

_____

_____

10. *How does this passage translate into our own lives? What kinds of things do we hold on to that perhaps we should consider "trash" compared to the value of knowing Christ?*

_____

_____

_____

_____

Paul jettisoned everything he once thought was important and rooted himself in Christ alone. Our roots matter. When we are rooted in transient things, our fruitfulness crumbles at the first sign of crisis. But when we're rooted in what can't be taken away from us and has surpassing worth—Jesus—we'll be able to thrive and grow no matter what.

The prophet Isaiah's words of hope to Hezekiah included these: "The surviving remnant of the house of Judah shall again take root downward and bear fruit upward" (Isaiah 37:31). The reason we can bear fruit even after a tragedy is because our roots still connect us with God, even if the surface of our lives has been ravaged. The deeper our roots are, the better they'll hold up in times of drought and storms and struggle.

Read Luke 8:5-6, 13.

[Jesus said,] "A sower went out to sow his seed. And as he sowed, some
fell along the path and was trampled underfoot, and the birds of the air
devoured it. And some fell on the rock, and as it grew up, it withered away,

because it had no moisture. . . . The ones on the rock are those who, when they hear the word, receive it with joy. But these have no root; they believe for a while, and in time of testing fall away."

11. *What happens to plants when they have no roots? What happens to believers who have shallow roots? Have you ever observed someone who fell away from their faith because their connection to God was not deep enough?*

Read Jeremiah 17:7-8.

Blessed is the one who trusts in the LORD,
    whose confidence is in him.
They will be like a tree planted by the water
    that sends out its roots by the stream.
It does not fear when heat comes;
    its leaves are always green.
It has no worries in a year of drought
    and never fails to bear fruit. (NIV)

12. *List the ways those who trust in the Lord thrive.*

_____

_____

_____

_____

13. *Do you feel that these verses describe you? If not, which of these descriptions would you most want to embrace?*

_____

_____

_____

_____

If roots are so important, the question becomes this: How do we deepen our roots? Read this beautiful passage from the apostle Paul in Ephesians 3:14-19:

> I bow my knees before the Father, from whom every family in heaven and on earth is named, that according to the riches of his glory he may grant you to be strengthened with power through his Spirit in your inner being, so that Christ may dwell in your hearts through faith—that you, being rooted and grounded in love, may have strength to comprehend with all the saints what is the breadth and length and height and depth, and to know the love of Christ that surpasses knowledge, that you may be filled with all the fullness of God.

14. *What does Paul say is the key nutrient that our roots need? What happens when we grasp the enormity of God's love for us?*

_____

_____

_____

_____

15. *What do you think it means to be "rooted and grounded in love"? In what practical ways does this affect how we live?*

_____

_____

_____

_____

In chapter 13, I write,

> I have come to believe that healthy, sustainable growth and immense fruit bearing feed from a single source: knowing we are immeasurably, immutably loved by Christ.

When this truth is more deeply rooted than any other belief we hold, even the fiercest tempest won't be able to rip us from the ground. Our leaves may be frayed and our branches bent, but our roots will hold fast.

But even long-time, faithful Christians sometimes lack this rootedness. In chapter 13, I talk about asking my ministry staff and the audience at a speaking event about their own most deeply held belief, the thing that they were most convinced was true. I wasn't asking for good Sunday school answers; I wanted to know what belief really informed everything these women did and the decisions they made.

Here are just a few of their answers:

This world will kill you, so stay on the run. If it catches you, you're dead.
Always be ready to jump. There's no room for relaxing. A shoe could drop at any time.
God always wants something different from what I want. If I really want it,
*   it won't be God's will. My desire jinxes what I'll get.*
Life is best lived under the radar. Don't be noticeable. Keep everything smooth.
*   Calm is the key.*
If people don't notice me, I'm not viable. Unseen equals unimportant.
I am responsible. I have to keep everything going, or it will all fall apart.
I have to be a success to be successful.
I am almost enough. If only I could be more or do just a little more.

16. **Do any of these responses strike a chord with you? Consider what your most deeply held belief is. If you're willing, share with the group.**

_____

_____

_____

17. **How might these and other false beliefs affect our faith, our choices, our relationships, our understanding of God, and our fruitfulness?**

_____

_____

_____

18. What might be the effect of replacing these false beliefs with a statement like "I am immeasurably, unconditionally loved by Christ"?

_____

_____

_____

_____

_____

It's not normal to believe any such thing. It's certainly not normal for this to be the belief you hold deepest of all. Such a belief is divine. It's muscular. It's protein, not carbohydrate. It requires "strength to comprehend . . . the breadth and length and height and depth, and to know the love of Christ that surpasses knowledge" (Ephesians 3:18-19). What if we sought the pure strength to comprehend how inconceivably loved we are? What if we sought that love like the marvel it really is?

That strength isn't something we come to possess all on our own; it's a "strength to comprehend *with all the saints*" (emphasis added). We need other strengthened saints to remind us that we are loved beyond any human estimate of breadth, length, height, and depth. When those around us forget, they need our strength to remind them of this truth.

19. How does your community of believers—whether that's your church, your small group, your family, or another group—remind you to remain rooted in God's love? How can you point someone else to the reality of God's love when they are struggling?

_____

_____

_____

_____

_____

PESTILENCE

We're moving from one of the most beautiful topics in all of faith—God's immense, unfailing love for us—to one of the most difficult: the reality of spiritual attack.

We don't like to think about it. You might even wonder why I wrote about it. I had to, because it's real. And if we ignore it or pretend it doesn't exist, then we are blindsided when it happens to us.

The devil hates when we are fruitful. That's why his attacks often come just at the time when we feel we've gained traction in our callings. We've found a way to serve Jesus that seems to be working, and then suddenly everything starts to fall apart. We feel as if somebody is against us. As I write in chapter 16,

> If the devil is doing his best work, you will think the somebody in question is God. There will be times you're convinced to your bones that God Himself is opposing the very thing He called you to do. Rather than believing that the One who called you is faithful to perform it (1 Thessalonians 5:24), you may feel like the One who called you is systematically, frustratingly *keeping* you from performing it.
>
> You might be tempted to think that God tricked you into something and then refused to support you. Or that He talked you into something beyond your natural abilities and then abandoned you, leaving you to fend for yourself.
>
> When the devil is doing a superb job, you may feel like God called you and then changed His mind about you, as if He didn't know who He was getting when He chose you.

1. *What lies are you tempted to believe about yourself when you feel attacked?*
   What lies are you tempted to believe about God? How might you counteract
   some of these lies?

   _____

   _____

   _____

   _____

Read 1 Thessalonians 5:23-24.

May the God of peace himself sanctify you completely, and may your whole spirit and soul and body be kept blameless at the coming of our Lord Jesus Christ. He who calls you is faithful; he will surely do it.

2. *What comfort can we take from these verses when we believe the lie that God has left us to fend for ourselves?*

_____

_____

_____

_____

Read Psalm 139:1-4.

O Lord, you have searched me and known me!
You know when I sit down and when I rise up;
   you discern my thoughts from afar.
You search out my path and my lying
     down
   and are acquainted with all my ways.
Even before a word is on my tongue,
   behold, O Lord, you know it
     altogether.

3. *How do these verses negate the lie that God might change His mind about us once He gets to know us better?*

_____

_____

_____

_____

Read 2 Thessalonians 1:11-12.

We keep on praying for you, asking our God to enable you to live a life
worthy of his call. May he give you the power to accomplish all the good
things your faith prompts you to do. Then the name of our Lord Jesus will
be honored because of the way you live, and you will be honored along with
him. This is all made possible because of the grace of our God and Lord,
Jesus Christ. (NLT)

4. *How does this passage counteract the lie that God might oppose or thwart our*
   callings?

_____

_____

_____

_____

Being on the receiving end of a spiritual attack can make us feel ashamed. Did we
bring this on ourselves? Are we being attacked because we were doing good work or
because we've done something wrong? Because we're unsure, we become ever more
isolated, embarrassed to admit what we're going through. But let me say it loud and
clear: you are not the only one.

What you may not realize is that every person worth his or her salt in the Kingdom
either has gone through their own version of the same thing or is enduring it this
very minute.

Read 1 Peter 5:8-11.

Be sober-minded; be watchful. Your adversary the devil prowls around
like a roaring lion, seeking someone to devour. Resist him, firm in your
faith, knowing that the same kinds of suffering are being experienced by
your brotherhood throughout the world. And after you have suffered a
little while, the God of all grace, who has called you to his eternal glory
in Christ, will himself restore, confirm, strengthen, and establish you.
To him be the dominion forever and ever. Amen.

5. How does Peter describe the devil? What helps us to resist him?

_____

_____

_____

_____

6. What ultimate hope does Peter point to?

_____

_____

_____

_____

7. As believers, how can we support each other better, knowing we all experience some amount of spiritual resistance? How can we pray for each other?

_____

_____

_____

_____

While we don't cause the devil's attacks, sometimes we can make them worse. In chapter 16, I write,

Satan can conserve significant energy if we'll simply enlist as our own worst enemy. This is good old-fashioned autosarcophagy: the practice of devouring one's own self.

When we turn the attacks inward, our vulnerabilities and our impressive abilities start erupting into liabilities. Our own hands take a crowbar to every crack in our armor.

Self-doubt, fear, condemnation, and blame are some common ways we turn the attack back on ourselves. Have you had any experience fighting these? If you're willing, share what helped you.

In chapter 16, I write,

What you're going through is how it goes for nearly everyone who's serious about serving Jesus. Now that you've come of age and had the faith and the audacity to bear much fruit, you have come of notice to the devil. Simultaneously, your unstoppably faithful God, who loves you immeasurably, has made a covenant at the Cross not only to save you but to conform you to the image of His Son.

Out of His exquisite grace, His obligation is to grow you up. And there is anguish in growing up. Among other things, growing up forces us to face the deceiver and pretender in our own mirror.

Doing this means looking honestly at our own past to see what patterns of sin might be making us vulnerable to the devil's attacks. This can be intensely personal, so we'll come back to it in the individual application section at the end of the chapter.

In chapter 16, I write,

The motto of the inexperienced is "Ignore the devil, and he'll go away." Nobody says that after a bloodbath. James says it this way: "Resist the devil, and he will flee from you" (4:7).

That's how this works. *Resist* is no passive term. It stands its ground, steel toed. It pushes back. It shoves hard. It applies divine might—a coat of armor, a sword in the right hand, and a shield in the left.

8. *How do we resist the devil? What specific things can we do when we are tempted to give in or give up? What resources or supports can we gather around us?*

_____

_____

_____

One of the best ways to resist the devil is to draw near to God, as James 4:8 says. We fill our minds with life-giving Scripture. We strive to remember God's constant presence with us. And we focus our minds on who He is, what He has done for us, and His power over anything that threatens us.

Read Romans 8:31-39.

What then shall we say to these things? If God is for us, who can be against us? He who did not spare his own Son but gave him up for us all, how will he not also with him graciously give us all things? Who shall bring any charge against God's elect? It is God who justifies. Who is to condemn? Christ Jesus is the one who died—more than that, who was raised—who is at the right hand of God, who indeed is interceding for us. Who shall separate us from the love of Christ? Shall tribulation, or distress, or persecution, or famine, or nakedness, or danger, or sword? . . .

No, in all these things we are more than conquerors through him who loved us. For I am sure that neither death nor life, nor angels nor rulers, nor things present nor things to come, nor powers, nor height nor depth, nor anything else in all creation, will be able to separate us from the love of God in Christ Jesus our Lord.

9. *List all the things Paul says are unable to separate us from God's love. What others would you add?*

_____

_____

_____

_____

10. *How can this passage encourage us when we feel condemned or under attack?*

_____

_____

_____

_____

In chapter 16, I write,

Coming of age is the most critical intersection of your calling. It's the place of Spirit and slaughter. It's the corner where you take one of two turns: either your fruitfulness will be devoured by the devil or your own flesh, or you will allow God to crucify your ego, fear, and lethargy and raise you to be immensely fruitful for His gospel.

If you're in a season of pestilence, fight it out. If you've gotten sloppy, tighten it up. If you're neck deep in sin, repent. Go back on your face before God. Open a Bible and plant your nose in it. Memorize Scripture. Learn how to fast and pray. Quit talking about Jesus more than you talk to Him. Quit letting your mouth overshoot your character. Become that person you've made fun of for taking Jesus too seriously. Live and love valiantly. Give generously. Help the poor.

You'll come out on the other side of every well-fought fight with something far better than an immense quantity of quality fruit. You'll come out knowing Jesus in a way you formerly believed He couldn't be known.

11. *If you're feeling discouraged today because of spiritual attack, what's one thing you can do to fight back? What's one piece of advice from this paragraph that you find helpful?*

_____

_____

_____

— *Wrapping Up* —

The two topics we've covered this week—roots and pestilence—may not seem to have much in common, but their connection is profound. Only deep roots in God's unimaginably lavish love can protect us from pestilence when it comes. Deep roots nourish us, anchor us, and help us to counteract the attacks of the devil. And deep roots allow us to be immensely fruitful.

What are we rooted in?

In chapter 13, I write,

Last year in a Q&A session, a young woman asked me a question I've
reflected on a hundred times since. "Beth, what is the knot in your rope?"
I'd never heard the question before. I knew my answer, but the thought
didn't escape me how recently it had come to be so.

    "It's John 15:9. Jesus said, 'As the Father has loved me, so have I loved you.'"

What's the knot in your rope? Let it be something that's worth it. Something that
can sustain you in any situation. Let it be the love of Christ.

— *Deepening Our Roots* —

On your own this week, try one or two of these activities:

- In a journal, write about what it means in your life that Jesus is "worth
  it" (see pages 79–80). How do His presence, His love, and His salvation
  overshadow all the struggles in our lives? If you're having trouble believing
  this is true, be honest with God about your doubts.
- Consider how you can grow your roots deeper into God's love. What spiritual
  disciplines might you practice to help you do so?
- Work on memorizing Ephesians 3:14-19, and let the truth about God's love
  sink deep in your soul.
- Reread the passage on page 90. What kinds of things in your past, your
  personality, or your tendencies do you need to address so you can "grow up"
  in faith and be better able to resist the attacks of the devil? How could you
  take a first step to deal with one of these things?
- Write out Romans 8:31-39 and hang it somewhere you'll see it frequently.
  Each time you read it, take a minute to consider what it means to be a
  conqueror in Jesus.

The Harvest

On this mountain the LORD Almighty will prepare
a feast of rich food for all peoples, a banquet of aged wine—
the best of meats and the finest of wines.

ISAIAH 25:6, NIV

GROUP GATHERING

Discussion: As a group, discuss your answers to the selected questions in the previous "On Your Own" section based on part 4, "The Fruit."

Watch session 5 of the DVD.

— *Listening Guide* —

1. What ideas or phrases in the DVD segment caught your attention?

_____

_____

_____

_____

2. Read 1 Peter 4:12:

Dear friends, do not be astonished that a trial by fire is occurring among you, as though something strange were happening to you. (NET)

Why can we be confident that we will never be destroyed?

_____

_____

_____

_____

3. Read Deuteronomy 26:8-11:

Then the LORD brought us out of Egypt with a strong hand and an outstretched arm, with terrifying power, and with signs and wonders. He led us to this place and gave us this land, a land flowing with milk and honey. I have now brought the first of the land's produce that you, LORD, have given me. You will then place the container before the LORD your God and bow down to him. You, the Levites, and the resident aliens among you will rejoice in all the good things the LORD your God has given you and your household. (CSB)

Write down the first three words of this passage:

_____ , _____ _____

— *Prayer* —

Take some time to share concerns with your group and pray together. Thank God for the joy you can experience when you see the fruit He is producing in your lives. Ask Him to show you how better to love and care for those around you—and to help you remember that there are no exceptions to His command to love. And pray that you will be able to remember the feast and celebration that are coming one day, when we will be able to fully experience our redemption and see all the ways God has made our lives full of meaning and good fruit.

+ + +

ON YOUR OWN

During the week, read part 5 ("The Harvest") of *Chasing Vines*. Then proceed with "A Word from Beth" and this week's homework. You're headed into your last week! Fully embrace what God has ahead for you. Enjoy it! I pray you're already seeing some fruit from the investment of your valuable time.

— A Word from Beth —

In the fifth part of *Chasing Vines*, "The Harvest," we arrive at the culmination of all this planting, cultivating, growing. It's the moment we have been waiting for: the fruit is ripe and ready for harvest!

In chapter 17, I write,

Imagine that it's dawn, and you and I have just pulled up to a vast, green vineyard on a rolling hillside. The grapes are at peak ripeness, shimmering in the dew. It's basket-grabbing season. But lest you slog onto that field heavy footed, looking like your dog just died, you need know that the harvest is boisterous. The work is hard, but the mood could hardly be lighter.

After all the laboring, rock clearing, hoeing, weeding, waiting, growing, staking, guarding, pruning, weather watching, and clock watching, the time has finally come for grape picking. And as it turns out, with grape picking comes partying.

— Planting the Seed —

INGATHERING

Those of us who don't live in agricultural societies may not understand the sheer joy that comes when the months of hard work culminate in a final harvest. The Lord reflected this joy when He commanded the Israelites to celebrate a harvest feast.

Read Deuteronomy 16:13-15.

You shall keep the Feast of Booths seven days, when you have gathered in the produce from your threshing floor and your winepress. You shall rejoice in your feast, you and your son and your daughter, your male servant and your female servant, the Levite, the sojourner, the fatherless, and the widow who are within your towns. For seven days you shall keep the feast to the LORD your God at the place that the LORD will choose, because the LORD your God will bless you in all your produce and in all the work of your hands, so that you will be altogether joyful.

1. *What were the people celebrating? Why do you think God put this feast in place?*

_____

_____

_____

_____

2. *What times of joy and celebration stand out in your life? Why were they meaningful to you?*

_____

_____

_____

_____

We sometimes think of joy as an anomaly—a rare, pleasant surprise in the midst of life that overflows with difficulty. But God intends rejoicing to be an integral part of life.

In chapter 17, I write,

God intended joy to be such a part of the harvest that, if it was missing, the people of God would know something was awry. Sustained joylessness was a red flag, an indicator for them to raise their chins and look to God for what had gone wrong.

The problem wasn't always direct disobedience. Sometimes an oppressive enemy was to blame. Either way, joy was never meant to be a hit-or-miss condition of the people of God. Joy was divinely determined to be one of a believer's most consistent and distinguishing features.

3. *Why do you think joy should characterize followers of Christ?*

_____

_____

_____

_____

4. *When do you experience joy? How do you define it?*

_____

_____

_____

_____

5. *Do you know someone who is notably joyful? How would you describe that person? What do you think is the source of their joy?*

_____

_____

_____

_____

Given how many times the Bible instructs us to rejoice, it's odd that some of us have bought into the idea that continually being serious is the more spiritual choice. In chapter 17, I write,

It's not a badge of maturity to sit back passively and refuse to take joy in our fruitfulness. We're meant to celebrate and kick up our heels a bit when the

Lord of the harvest brings fruit from our labors. When we act as if we don't notice God's blessings, it's not humility. It's ingratitude.

Read Isaiah 51:3.

The LORD comforts Zion;
    he comforts all her waste places
and makes her wilderness like Eden,
    her desert like the garden of
        the LORD;
joy and gladness will be found
        in her,
    thanksgiving and the voice
        of song.

Read Psalm 126:3, 5-6.

The LORD has done great things
        for us;
    we are glad. . . .

Those who sow in tears
    shall reap with shouts of joy!
He who goes out weeping,
    bearing the seed for sowing,
shall come home with shouts of joy,
    bringing his sheaves with him.

6. List some things that are contrasted in these two passages.

_____

_____

_____

_____

7. *What is the response in each passage to God's work of producing growth and harvest?*

_____

_____

_____

We can rejoice in the harvest we see now—the fruit God is producing in our lives—as well as in the harvest we are promised in the future. Read 1 Peter 1:6-9.

So be truly glad. There is wonderful joy ahead, even though you must endure many trials for a little while. These trials will show that your faith is genuine. It is being tested as fire tests and purifies gold—though your faith is far more precious than mere gold. So when your faith remains strong through many trials, it will bring you much praise and glory and honor on the day when Jesus Christ is revealed to the whole world.

You love him even though you have never seen him. Though you do not see him now, you trust him; and you rejoice with a glorious, inexpressible joy. The reward for trusting him will be the salvation of your souls. (NLT)

8. *What is the ultimate reason we can rejoice in God? What is our ability to rejoice based on?*

_____

_____

_____

9. *How can we encourage one another with the idea that we are moving toward the harvest?*

_____

_____

_____

Both the passage from 1 Peter and Psalm 126 talk about joy following sorrow or trials.

10. *Have you had experiences when great joy came on the heels of great sorrow or difficulty? Why do you think this is?*

_____

_____

_____

_____

11. *How does sorrow make joy more precious?*

_____

_____

_____

_____

Joy is an integral part of the harvest because we see before us the beautiful evidence of what God has done and what we have had a part in producing. We rejoice to see the difference God has made in the world around us and how He has made our lives meaningful and productive.

A second integral part of the harvest is community. The grapes are harvested best when people work together.

In chapter 17, I write,

Time was of the essence for the ingathering. Wait even a few days too long, and ripe grapes start to wither and rot, skins popping, splitting, or shriveling. The Israelites had to move fast, and the bigger the vineyard, the more laborers were required. Entire villages were often involved in the picking, and booths pocked the vineyard's edge.

Men, women, and children moved rhythmically up and down the rows, baskets in hand, singing, dancing, and rejoicing. They shouted to one another over splendid clusters, celebrating with unbridled conviviality the goodness of God in bringing fruit from the dust of the earth.

Everyone was invited to participate.

Isn't this a beautiful picture of the Kingdom of God? Everyone is working together for a common goal, joyfully celebrating what God has done. No one can claim to have manufactured the grapes on their own, so there's no need for boasting. And the harvested grapes are available for all, so there's no need to make sure we have as much as the next person. We all have enough. What a taste of freedom!

12. *When have you been part of a team where the individual players were able to put aside their egos and differences to work together toward a common goal? What was the result?*

_____

_____

_____

_____

In chapter 17, I write,

We who are in Christ are never happier than when we're celebrating a harvest in community.

When the Holy Spirit is abundant and active in us, we don't care much who has gathered the most fruit at reaping time. We were all part of the vintage year, moving up and down those rows together at the Feast of Ingathering. The credit for a great harvest goes to the Vinedresser, but the glee abounds to all.

The apostle Paul addressed this idea when he wrote to the believers in Corinth, who were dividing their allegiances based on who had led them to Christ. Read 1 Corinthians 3:5-7.

What then is Apollos? What is Paul? Servants through whom you believed, as the Lord assigned to each. I planted, Apollos watered, but God gave the growth. So neither he who plants nor he who waters is anything, but only God who gives the growth.

13. *What was the shared goal of both Paul and Apollos? How did this keep them from being concerned about the other's success?*

_____

_____

_____

Human nature can lead to envy and jealousy of other people's ministry, success, or gifts. This makes sense when our goals are individual success and getting the most accolades. But in the context of the body of believers, our approach should be radically different.

Read Romans 12:3-8.

Don't think you are better than you really are. Be honest in your evaluation of yourselves, measuring yourselves by the faith God has given us. Just as our bodies have many parts and each part has a special function, so it is with Christ's body. We are many parts of one body, and we all belong to each other.

In his grace, God has given us different gifts for doing certain things well. So if God has given you the ability to prophesy, speak out with as much faith as God has given you. If your gift is serving others, serve them well. If you are a teacher, teach well. If your gift is to encourage others, be encouraging. If it is giving, give generously. If God has given you leadership ability, take the responsibility seriously. And if you have a gift for showing kindness to others, do it gladly. (NLT)

14. *Why do envy and jealousy have no place among believers? What is the significance of believers being part of one body?*

_____

_____

_____

15. How can we live out the instructions in verses 6-8? What should our focus be?

_____

_____

_____

_____

If we are using our own gifts to the best of our ability, we won't have time to look at someone else and wish we had their gifts. And when we acknowledge that we are one body, we recognize that we're on the same team. If someone else uses their gift to share the gospel, the whole body benefits! If another person uses his gifts to serve, the whole body benefits! As Ephesians 4:16 says, "[Christ] makes the whole body fit together perfectly. As each part does its own special work, it helps the other parts grow, so that the whole body is healthy and growing and full of love" (NLT). There is joy in seeing God produce good fruit in others and knowing that we are a part of the same abundant harvest.

In chapter 17, I quote Dr. R. H. Strachan's words about joy:

> The *joy* of Jesus is the joy that arises from the sense of a finished work. It is creative joy, like the joy of the artist. It produces a sense of unexhausted power for fresh creation. This joy in the heart of Jesus is both the joy of victory ([John] 15:11), and the sense of having brought His church into being.[*]

16. What work has already been finished in Christ? What work is being finished in us?

_____

_____

_____

_____

[*] R. H. Strachan, *The Fourth Gospel* (London: Student Christian Movement Press, 1955), quoted in Leon Morris, *The Gospel according to John* (Grand Rapids, MI: Eerdmans, 1995), 598.

17. Take time as a group to celebrate some moments of harvest. What fruit in each other's lives can you recognize and rejoice over? Tell someone else what you see God producing in him or her.

_____

_____

_____

_____

GLEANINGS

The joy of the harvest is too good not to share.

Some people think Leviticus is a dry and boring book of the Bible. I'll admit it has its moments (skin diseases, anyone?), but it's also filled with kernels of truth that reveal the heart of God. One of those comes in Leviticus 19:9-10:

> When you reap the harvest of your land, you shall not reap your field right up to its edge, neither shall you gather the gleanings after your harvest. And you shall not strip your vineyard bare, neither shall you gather the fallen grapes of your vineyard. You shall leave them for the poor and for the sojourner: I am the LORD your God.

The "gleanings" were the parts of the harvest left behind after the workers had made their first pass through the fields or the vineyards. These were to be left for "the sojourner, the fatherless, and the widow" (Deuteronomy 24:19). The Israelites are told that they should follow this practice because they were once slaves in Egypt and "the LORD your God redeemed you from there" (Deuteronomy 24:18).

1. What do these passages reveal about God's character and priorities?

_____

_____

_____

_____

2. *How do you think remembering their own slavery and redemption would prompt the Israelites to follow these commands to care for the poor?*

_____

_____

_____

_____

The Lord made sure that the joy of the harvest was not limited to those who owned the land. It was to spill over to those who were easily forgotten and overlooked.

God commanded the Israelites to leave behind the fruit on the edges of the field, where it would be simpler for the poor and widowed to find and gather. He wanted to encourage His people to embrace a level of compassion beyond anything they would have on their own. I write in chapter 18, "As God often does, He called His people to a reversal of natural tendency—both as a service to others and as a way to set them apart from the world. 'Make it easy for those in need. Make their provision plain to see.'"

3. *Where in your life have you found that following Christ meant nurturing a "reversal of natural tendency"—in other words, learning to do something contrary to your natural inclination? In what ways is this difficult for you?*

_____

_____

_____

_____

Read Romans 8:5-6.

Those who live according to the flesh have their minds set on what the flesh desires; but those who live in accordance with the Spirit have their minds set on what the Spirit desires. The mind governed by the flesh is death, but the mind governed by the Spirit is life and peace. (NIV)

4. *What contrast does this passage highlight between living according to the flesh and living according to the Spirit? How do we benefit from countering some of our natural tendencies for the sake of following Christ?*

_____

_____

_____

_____

God still calls us to a level of compassion far beyond what we would have on our own. And we can always find people around us who are in need of the grace and loving care that only the people of God can give.

Take a look at the edges of our fields, and you'll see people our society claims don't matter. But in God's eyes, every soul is of inestimable worth. And these people at the edges of the field are hungry. Hungry for love. Hungry for affection. Hungry for friendship. Hungry for a listening ear. Hungry for hope. Hungry to know God is there and that He cares. And I wonder—have we harvested with the margins in mind? Do we intentionally serve people on the edge?

We have gleaned such grace from the Vinedresser's field. "Freely you have received," Jesus said. "Freely give" (Matthew 10:8, NIV).

5. *Who in your life might be hanging around the edges of the field, looking for sustenance, friendship, or hope? What could you do—individually or as a group—to reach out to one of these people?*

_____

_____

_____

_____

_____

6. *In what situations is it easy for you to be compassionate toward others? When is it more difficult?*

_____

_____

_____

In the story of Ruth, which I discuss in chapter 18, we see that Ruth received far more than she asked for—or perhaps even more than she thought she needed. She came to the field looking for enough food to keep herself and Naomi alive. She received not only more food than the two of them could eat but also a husband, a home, a family, a child, and a new sense of belonging. That's the lavish, abundant, generous grace of our Lord.

We, too, are given much more than we could ever expect by a generous God. Read Ephesians 1:6-8.

We praise God for the glorious grace he has poured out on us who belong to his dear Son. He is so rich in kindness and grace that he purchased our freedom with the blood of his Son and forgave our sins. He has showered his kindness on us, along with all wisdom and understanding. (NLT)

7. *What language is used in this passage to underscore God's generosity? List the things He has given us.*

_____

_____

_____

8. *In light of all we have been given, how can we turn that generosity toward others?*

_____

_____

_____

Read 2 Corinthians 9:6-11.

Remember this: Whoever sows sparingly will also reap sparingly, and whoever sows generously will also reap generously. Each of you should give what you have decided in your heart to give, not reluctantly or under compulsion, for God loves a cheerful giver. And God is able to bless you abundantly, so that in all things at all times, having all that you need, you will abound in every good work. As it is written:

"They have freely scattered their gifts to the poor;
    their righteousness endures forever."

Now he who supplies seed to the sower and bread for food will also supply and increase your store of seed and will enlarge the harvest of your righteousness. You will be enriched in every way so that you can be generous on every occasion, and through us your generosity will result in thanksgiving to God. (NIV)

9. *Why do you think those who sow generously will also reap generously? How do God's abundance and provision affect our ability to be generous?*

_____

_____

_____

_____

Generosity doesn't only encompass money or material things. Think of someone you know who is generous with their time, home, presence, or love. What are the results of their generosity? What do you think motivates them?

Sometimes money is the easiest thing to give. But God's call to love our neighbors requires us to give more—to give of ourselves.

In chapter 18, I retell the story of the Good Samaritan, putting you in the place of the injured man. When you realize that someone from a group you've reviled in the past has come to your aid, you're shocked and confused.

Reread this story on your own and then consider: If you were to set the story in today's culture, who would be the Samaritan? What person (or group of people) would you least expect to care generously for you—whether because of your own behavior toward them in the past or because of your assumptions about what they are like? How does it feel to imagine the story with that person or group in mind?

10. *Why is it so difficult to love our enemies or people we don't understand? What stands in our way?*

_____

_____

_____

_____

11. *When Jesus told His hearers to "go and do likewise," how do you think they responded?*

_____

_____

_____

_____

Jesus' teaching in this parable was shocking to His hearers because He turned conventional thinking on its head. He told His listeners—who included teachers of the law who believed they perfectly understood and followed God's law—to love like a Samaritan. How could He suggest that someone who didn't have a proper pedigree or an accurate understanding of Jewish law could love God and their neighbor better than they did themselves?

Here's the reality: some of the Pharisees loved only people who were like them—and only when it was convenient. The Samaritan in the story went far out of his way to care for someone who hated him.

Read Matthew 5:43-46.

You have heard that it was said, "You shall love your neighbor and hate your enemy." But I say to you, Love your enemies and pray for those who persecute you, so that you may be sons of your Father who is in heaven. For he makes his sun rise on the evil and on the good, and sends rain on the just and on the unjust. For if you love those who love you, what reward do you have? Do not even the tax collectors do the same?

This is a familiar passage that's easy to gloss over, but take a moment to think about who our "enemies" might be.

12. *What types of people might Christians today think of as enemies or opponents? If we followed Jesus' instructions, how might our approach to these people change?*

_____

_____

_____

_____

_____

_____

Read 1 Peter 4:8.

Above all, keep loving one another earnestly, since love covers a multitude of sins.

Read Colossians 3:12-14.

Put on then, as God's chosen ones, holy and beloved, compassionate hearts, kindness, humility, meekness, and patience, bearing with one another and, if one has a complaint against another, forgiving each other; as the Lord has forgiven you, so you also must forgive. And above all these put on love, which binds everything together in perfect harmony.

13. *What specific words or phrases are used in these passages to describe the way believers should treat one another?*

_____

_____

_____

_____

14. *Based on these passages, what are some of the results of loving others?*

_____

_____

_____

_____

15. *How do you think love changes both those who love and those who are loved?*

_____

_____

_____

_____

In chapter 18, I write,

Love God. Love people. That's what we're here to do. "The fruit of the Spirit is love" (Galatians 5:22). Without love, all fruit is plastic. The fruit of our lives, in all its forms and manifold graces, is truest to the Vine when it's generously extended and accessible to strangers and aliens of any kind.

Our fruit is sweetest to the Vine when it extends a direct advantage to the disadvantaged and to the orphan, to the widow and to the poor. Our fruit best reflects the Vine when it deliberately leaves room at the edges—for the marginalized, the cornered, the oppressed, the mistreated, the harassed, and the abused. That's where Jesus went, and that's who Jesus sought. "As he is so also are we in this world" (1 John 4:17).

16. *Who are the marginalized, oppressed, poor, and hurting around us? How can we reach out to them with genuine love?*

Our love for others is not genuine if it has an ulterior motive. Those who have a passion for the gospel will of course desire to see others come to faith in Christ. However, we must love others—both believers and those who are not—because they are people created in God's image, not because we hope our love will bring them to faith.

In chapter 18, I tell the story of my brother, who has been a Buddhist for many years. Our relationship grew warmer again when we began to ask questions about the other's beliefs and to talk openly about our own—with no agendas or hidden motives, but simply with a desire to understand the other's point of view. I write, "He hasn't embraced Christianity, but I can tell you this: he no longer thinks Jesus is a jerk."

17. *Have you encountered a similar situation with a friend or family member who was hostile to your faith? How did you handle it? What kinds of responses were helpful and which were not?*

_____

_____

_____

_____

In chapter 18, I write,

It's possible to love in deed and do good to others, neither flaunting nor hiding our identity. . . . [Jesus said,] "This is to my Father's glory, that you bear much fruit, showing yourselves to be my disciples" (John 15:8, NIV). We are not called to be showy, but make no mistake: we are called to be showing.

18. *How can we show our fruit and our identity as followers of Christ?*

_____

_____

_____

Read 1 Peter 2:12.

Maintain good conduct among the non-Christians, so that though they now malign you as wrongdoers, they may see your good deeds and glorify God when he appears. (NET)

19. How could we do better at maintaining "good conduct" around our nonbelieving friends and neighbors?

Deep inside, we all want to do good to other people. We know that we, too, were once wanderers. We, too, were once slaves. We, too, were once poor in spirit. But now, in Christ, we have found a home. We have been set free. We have been made rich.

We may not be owners, bosses, or managers, and we may not be wealthy or well known, but we possess more authority than we recognize. We put it to use in our neighborhoods, in our children's schools, in our churches, in civic matters, in social issues, and on social media. Any place we have influence, we utilize a measure of authority.

If we're exercising this authority as imitators of Christ, we don't do so as bullies who are strong-arming others in the name of Jesus. Rather, we're acting as influencers of good, identifiable by the kindness of Christ.

20. How does recognizing what we once were, and knowing who we are now in Christ, give us motivation to love everyone—neighbors, enemies, political opponents—with no exceptions? How can we be "influencers of good"?

_____

_____

_____

— *Wrapping Up* —

This week I want to leave you with a glimpse of the culmination of the harvest: the great feast we will one day experience in heaven, when God has redeemed His people and His creation. Reflect on this incredible picture of the future from Isaiah:

On this mountain the LORD Almighty will
    prepare
  a feast of rich food for all peoples,
a banquet of aged wine—
    the best of meats and the finest of wines.
On this mountain he will destroy
    the shroud that enfolds all peoples,
the sheet that covers all nations;
    he will swallow up death forever.
The Sovereign LORD will wipe away
      the tears
    from all faces;
he will remove his people's disgrace
    from all the earth.
The LORD has spoken.

In that day they will say,

"Surely this is our God;
    we trusted in him, and he saved us.
This is the LORD, we trusted in him;
    let us rejoice and be glad in his
      salvation."

ISAIAH 25:6-9, NIV

No more death. No more tears. No more disgrace or shame or condemnation. No more rocks in the soil, no more pruning or pestilence, no more transplanting, no more rotten fruit.

Only good fruit. Abundant harvest. Feasting. Abiding in Christ—actually experiencing His presence—in a way we can't even imagine now.

And when we look back, we'll see the fruit God has produced in us, and we'll know that none of it was wasted.

May this joy be ours.

— *Deepening Our Roots* —

On your own this week, try one or two of these activities:

- In a journal, reflect on the fruit God has already harvested in your life. Rejoice over what He has produced in you, and be encouraged as you think about His work in the future.
- Identify where you might be envious of someone else's gifts or accomplishments. Reread Romans 12:3-8 and consider what it means to be different parts of the body of Christ, with a common goal.
- In a Bible concordance, look up *joy* or *rejoice*. Write one or two verses that remind you of the role joy should play in the lives of believers.
- Memorize Colossians 3:12-14 and meditate on what it means to "put on love."
- Think about the people in your church, community, or social circle who might be in need. How can you reach out to someone who might be on the fringes? Choose one practical way to show generosity this week.
- Find a song or hymn that reminds you of our hope of heaven, and listen to it throughout the week.

A Fruitful Life

By this my Father is glorified, that you bear much fruit
and so prove to be my disciples. . . . You did not choose me, but I chose you
and appointed you that you should go and bear fruit
and that your fruit should abide.

JOHN 15:8, 16

GROUP GATHERING

Note to leaders: If time permits, consider having a celebration as part of your final session. What could be more appropriate than a feast of some kind? I wish I could be there with all of you. Know that I am there in spirit!

Discussion: As a group, discuss your answers to the selected questions in the previous "On Your Own" section based on part 5, "The Harvest."

Watch session 6 of the DVD.

— *Listening Guide* —

1. What ideas or phrases in the DVD segment caught your attention?

_____

_____

_____

2. *Share about a meaningful communion experience. What made that experience stand out?*

_____

_____

_____

_____

_____

— Prayer —

Take some time to share concerns with your group and pray together. Thank God for the way He loves us just as we are but doesn't leave us there. Ask Him to continue to nurture you so you bear much fruit. And pray that He will use you as He reaps a great harvest for His eternal Kingdom.

✦　✦　✦

ON YOUR OWN

— Wrapping Up —

Over the past six sessions, we've looked at what it means to make our lives matter by bearing fruit. We've looked at the process of growing—from planting, to soil, to seeds, to roots, and finally, to the joyful harvest. I hope you have gotten a glimpse of what it means to abide in Christ as a branch of His vine—to be so connected with Him, so dependent on Him, that He produces fruit in us that we could never produce on our own. And we've discovered the joy of the harvest—the way the master Gardener loves to celebrate and invites us to do the same.

Take some time to read the epilogue and reflect on what you've learned over the course of this study.

- What are some of the key takeaways you've gleaned from the book, the videos, and the discussions?
- What Scripture passages have come to life in a new way?
- What would you like to change in your day-to-day life as a result of what you've learned?
- What's one step you can take this week toward a more fruitful life?

ABOUT THE AUTHOR

Author and speaker Beth Moore is a dynamic teacher whose conferences take her across the globe. Beth founded Living Proof Ministries in 1994 with the purpose of encouraging women to know and love Jesus through the study of Scripture. She has written numerous bestselling books and Bible studies, including *Breaking Free*, *Believing God*, *Entrusted*, and *The Quest*, which have been read by women of all ages, races, and denominations. Another recent addition includes her first work of fiction, *The Undoing of Saint Silvanus*.

Beth recently celebrated twenty years of Living Proof Live conferences. She can be seen teaching Bible studies on the television program *Living Proof with Beth Moore*, aired on the Trinity Broadcasting Network.

She and her husband of forty years reside in Houston, Texas. She is a dedicated wife, the mother of two adult daughters, and the grandmother of three delightful grandchildren.

Join Beth on her journey of discovering what it means to chase vines— and learn how to fully embrace God's amazing design for a fruitful, abundant, and meaningful life.

Chasing Vines: Popular teacher and speaker Beth Moore helps us understand how our life—and our relationship with God—could be different if we better understood and fully embraced His amazing design for making fruitful lives that matter.

Chasing Vines DVD Experience: Designed for use with the *Chasing Vines Group Experience,* this six-session DVD curriculum based on Beth Moore's book explores the ways God delights in watching things grow—and how the land of the vineyard holds the secret for how we can have a fruitful life.

Chasing Vines Group Experience: This is a six-session workbook designed for use with the *Chasing Vines DVD Experience,* based on the book by Beth Moore. A great resource for church groups, Bible studies, and anyone who's ever wondered how God makes everything in life matter!

Promises for a Fruitful Life: Drawn from Scripture and passages from Beth Moore's book *Chasing Vines,* this booklet will help you find new hope for Kingdom building. With each page, you'll be reminded that your life matters— and nothing you've experienced will be wasted by the One who created you.

To learn more from Beth and access additional resources, visit her online at Bethmoore.org.

CP1547